MAKE MONEY WITH ADULT WEBSITES

A Guide to the Adult Internet Business
and How To Profit from Internet Sites

By Jack Spriggs

Venture Books

Venture Books

Copyright © 2008 by Jack Spriggs. All rights reserved.

ISBN 978-1-4357-0848-8

Table of Contents

Getting Started in a Money Making Business	4
A Brief History of Internet Porn	8
Types of Adult Sites - Where the Money Is	14
General vs. Niche Content	23
Sponsor/Affiliate Programs	27
Locating Content	36
Domain Names	43
Hosting	50
A Model Website	55
Source Code for Warning Page	65
Source Code for Main Page	71
Source Code for Gallery Page	73
Some Thoughts About HTML Coding	75
Sources of Traffic	79
Hardware and Software	91
Backing Up Your Site	101
Taxes and Other Business Matters	104
Glossary of Adult Terms	108
Getting Help	114

Getting Started in a Money Making Business

About two years ago, I picked up a magazine on an airport newsstand. It's subject was how to become a successful seller on eBay. Since I was naturally interested in making money, I bought the magazine and started reading. It contained numerous "feel-good articles" about people who had found their way to riches or at least decent second incomes through eBay auctions. One that I particularly remember was about a nineteen-year-old fellow who had great success selling baby strollers. He made $80,000 in sales the first year and was expecting to make several hundred thousand a year in the near future.

This article piqued my interest. How could a nineteen-year-old be successful so fast? Upon close reading, I realized the article doesn't claim that he made $80,000 profit. There is a big difference between gross income from sales and the amount left over after paying for the strollers, shipping, and business operation expenses. Perhaps his profit was very small and not really worth the effort expended. In addition, the several hundred thousand a year figure was just speculation. If there really is that much demand for baby strollers over the Internet, then wouldn't better funded competitors be quick to jump in and take away sales?

That magazine and the countless books on how to be successful with eBay are simply examples of why one needs to thoroughly research a potential profit-making venture before jumping in. I sensed that this was true from my previous business ventures. So, I decided to invest a small amount of cash (about $100) and my time to investigate whether I could make money on eBay. I bought a couple of books along the lines of the "...for Dummies" titles for about $25 each. Both books dealt primarily with eBay as a business venture. I also studied the excellent help topics on the eBay website that provide how-to instructions for sellers. By registering as an eBay member, I was able to view the sales records of specific auction items.

For example, I looked up a popular digital SLR camera that I owned to see how well it would sell. I found many auctions. Some sold. Many didn't. There were many competitors trying to sell the same merchandise. One guy might offer the used camera for $399. Another guy would deliberately (I think) offer the same camera for $395 hoping to get the sale. From this, I realized that competition may be a factor that I hadn't considered.

In the end, I faced one nagging detail: I didn't have anything in mind that I might sell. After you sell all the old junk out of your garage and basement, what do you really sell? I looked at eBay discussion groups and found that a lot of other people were asking the same question. In fact, there are whole websites devoted to helping you find products to sell. I bought one more book for about $40 that dealt specifically with how to find products to sell. It was a good book, but when I got done I still had nothing in mind that would be marketable and produce a worthwhile profit.

The end of the story is that I didn't go into eBay sales. My $100 was extremely well-spent! Research had saved me from spending thousands of dollars getting started in some ill-conceived venture. Like many Internet startups, I could have spent months trying to market some product that someone told me was the next great thing.

The moral of the story is that you need to research carefully before jumping into any business. Being an adult webmaster requires research, too. The purpose of this book is to give you information that you need in order to make an informed decision as to whether you want to invest your time and money in this field.

I started as an adult webmaster in the nineties. I was already knowledgeable about computers and HTML programming. Still, there were a lot of questions. How would I obtain a domain name (URL) for my site? How would I go about finding a good hosting company? Where would I get pictures of naked girls (content) for my pages? And how, exactly, would all of this lead to making money? In this book I have tried to answer these questions and more just as I faced them in the nineties. That era is sometimes referred to as "the golden age of porn". It was incredibly easy to start making money because there was a limited amount of competition. As described earlier, guys were just getting their first computers with Internet connections and anxious to sign up through AOL and other sources   There was a certain naivety and innocence about the whole thing. Things have changed to some extent. The "golden age" is past.

      To be successful, one needs to develop quality sites and get lots of traffic (surfers) to visit your site.   Making money is still possible. A realistic approach as to what one can do in a productive manner and applying good business principles are the secrets to success in this endeavor. I truly hope this book will help you to develop a path to success.

                    Jack Spriggs

A Brief History of Internet Porn

Pornography has existed in various forms for hundreds, if not thousands, of years. Its method of delivery has changed from ancient crude stone carvings and drawings to modern DVD disks, the Internet, and even handheld devices such as cell phones. The history of modern pornography begins about 1994 with the rise of the Internet as a delivery method. The Internet had previously been used primarily by government, educational, and research institutions. About 1994 several developments made the Internet available to ordinary people in their homes and offices:

1. The invention of the web browser, especially Netscape that received Internet messages in HTML (hypertext markup language) and converted them to text and images.

2. The rise of business web-hosting companies that provided servers for commercial purposes including adult content.

3. The decision of several companies such as AOL (America Online) and CompuServe to switch from modem-based telephone-line connections to the Internet.

4. The rise of modern credit card billing methods which enabled websites to charge for services that were rendered over the net rather than physical delivery of a product through the mail.

The first Internet sites were crude by today's standards. Netscape used a grey screen background by default with black text. Links appeared in blue or dark red depending upon whether they had been clicked or not. Pages were mainly text-oriented with few photos or other graphics because it was inherently slow to transmit images files. Most users were connected from home via modems with transmission speeds of 1200 or 2400 baud that were painfully slow. Over the late 90's, these modem speeds increased to 9600, 14400, and 28000 baud. Businesses had connections using dedicated T1, partial T1, or T3 lines which were many times faster than telephone lines. The gradual increase in transmission speed was instrumental in the rise of Internet based porn. Webmasters were finally able to deliver photos, typically of naked girls, at acceptable speeds.

Commercial web hosting companies for the most part shunned porn sites. Many had specific prohibitions on adult-type content not so much for moral or ethical reasons but because these sites attracted enormous amounts of web traffic that bogged down their servers. There was also a perception that porn webmasters were somehow an unsavory and un-business-like group of individuals who were on the verge of illegality in their operations. Gradually over the 90's, servers gained speed and the connections using modern fiber optic cable took away most of the physical restrictions that had limited web porn development. Pornography became big business run by men in suits who started major companies with multi-million dollar financial backing. Porn or near-porn became an acceptable part of our society.

In the early 90's, there are a number of companies that offered group networks for purposes of discussion and sharing of files. Some of the largest were AOL and CompuServe which later merged. These companies along with large telecom companies such as AT&T Worldnet and MCI began to actively market their Internet connection products. Though deals with computer manufacturers, these companies were able to offer their products already installed on the desktops of modern Windows computers. As word spread about the availability of porn Internet sites, many guys bought computers for the first time in the late 90's. They quickly signed up for AOL or one of its competitors and typed "porn" into a search program. Thus began the rise of commercial porn as opposed to just a bunch of guys sharing their "dirty pictures".

As a commercial product, pornography could not have grown without a method of converting picture delivery to cash. Credit cards such as MasterCard and Visa were operated by the major banks, and the bankers had no desire to align themselves with porn merchants. This was due not only to public pressure, but also because of specific problems with charge-backs that commonly arose with porn websites.

A charge-back means that the customer asks the credit card company to reverse a specific charge and send it back through the billing system so the customer's account receives a credit.

There was already a general concern about security issues when charging anything over the Internet. Ability to accept any credit card purchases required that the business open a "merchant account" with a bank. Banks were more apt to open accounts with brick and mortar businesses that sold actual physical products. Porn webmasters had the problem that their product was the transmission of pictures instead of physical merchandise. The solution to this dilemma came in the rise of billing companies. These companies took over the billing details by signing up for merchant accounts themselves, and then handling the billing details for webmasters. Companies such as CCBill, Epoch, and Ibill handled the processing details so individual webmasters didn't have to sign up for merchant accounts through their own banks. Due to the volume of transactions, these companies had some clout with merchant banks and were better able to deal with the problems that arise from online transactions.

In the earliest porn sites, a person might buy sets of pictures that were downloaded over a modem - a painfully slow process. That business model quickly fell aside to the concept of the membership site. Here, the buyer purchases a "membership" which usually runs for one month at a time that is billed on a credit card. During the month, the purchaser is free to log in and view the content anytime. Photos can usually be downloaded to the user's computer with a click of the mouse. Likewise, a modern video file can be viewed as streaming content with no attempt at permanent download, or it can be downloaded to the user's computer.

At first, site membership was for one month at a time, but soon the billing sites worked out the concept of the recurring monthly membership. Each membership keeps getting automatically renewed each month unless the member takes the required steps to cancel. This model prevails today even though it has brought about many complaints of fraud and was generally resisted by the banks because it results in high charge-backs. Complaints and threats of prosecution have caused many porn webmasters and billing sites to clean up their acts. Today, the customer support at most billing sites will be willing cancel a membership if requested for almost any reason just to avoid the cost of a charge-back.

Beginning about the year 2000 there are several major developments and new directions in Internet porn:

1. A switch to "reality" content.

2. Less emphasis on delivery of photographs and more emphasis on video content.

3. Legal challenges to underage performers.

As said above, the first site content featured photos of naked models. In the 90's, these pictures were small by today's standards due to the slowness of transmission. Typical photos might be 300x400 pixels which were viewed on a computer monitor with 480x640 resolution. In the 2000's, as the monitor resolution grew to 1280x1024 and more, the size of photos also had to grow so that nowadays a photo that fills the screen might have a size of 1000 pixels or more. A typical porn webpage might consist of a series of photos of a single model that were posed and shot in a studio or outdoor setting.

After 2000, there as a shift to scenarios that suggested a more realistic setting or live performance. These reality sites conveyed a short, if improbable, story. For example: a guy comes to an apartment to deliver a pizza. Two hot girls answer the door. They quickly become involved in a hardcore sex scene with the guy. The gist of these scene-oriented stories is limited only by the pornographer's imagination. With reality sites came a shift in camera styles. Scenes were shot in a candid mode as if the camera is looking in on some normal sexual activity instead of a posed scene. A POV (point-of-view) style often implies that the photographer, himself, is participating in the sexual activity while holding the camera in one hand.

The development of modern video techniques as related to the Internet is greatly indebted to porn developers. Many of the advanced video features such as streaming video were first offered by the porn webmasters in order to satisfy the need to feature live content. Also, porn needed to compete with adult DVD sales that were rapidly growing. Streaming content delivery even enables porn sites to deliver DVD type material on a pay-per-view basis. In most pay site operations, there has been a gradual shift from a primary focus on photographs to more and more video content after the year 2000.

Finally, there have been major changes in the legal aspects of Internet pornography. The Clinton administration chose not to focus on prosecuting porn creators for a variety of reasons. Mainly, they were too busy with other matters. The more conservative Bush administration quickly ordered Attorneys General Ashcroft and Gonzales to seek out cases for prosecution. A major concern for webmasters has been enforcement of the so-called 2257 laws. These laws refer to Title 18 Section 2257 of the US Code (18 USC 2257) which deals with business records that must be kept by content producers. The main purpose of these laws is to prevent use of underage persons in pornography (under age 18).

Primary content producers are photographers, etc. who are actually involved in the filming of models. These producers are required to keep records as to the models' name, address, and proof-of-age documents at a stated place of business where they can be examined by the Federal authorities. In addition, sites are required to place a 2257 statement with information about these documents in a prominent place on the site. In general, porn webmasters have not been thought to fall under this law because usually they do not produce the content of their sites. Instead, they purchase content from photographers or content brokers making them "secondary producers".

Under the Bush administration, the 2257 laws were recently changed to make them applicable to secondary producers in addition. How this will play out may take years to decide. All laws passed by Congress are subject to interpretation by the courts which must take them into consideration in light of laws such as the US Constitution. While nobody wants to promote child porn, the courts must consider the effects of well-meaning legislators who pass overly broad statutes as do-all, be-all cures to the perceived injustices in this world. The final resolution of these issues is yet to be seen. The decisions in various future court cases may or may not have a profound effect on Internet porn.

Types of Adult Sites - Where the Money Is

Let's get started by looking at some different types of adult websites. Remember that our purpose here is to determine which ones can be profitable for the solo webmaster just starting out.

As a beginner, you also need a venture that doesn't cost an arm and leg in startup expenses. My original startup expenses were about $500. In those days photo content cost a whole lot more than it does now. A CD with six sets of photos of naked girls might cost $150-200. Nowadays, you can get a set of perfectly acceptable photos for as little as $10. There are even sources of free content. However, we won't dwell on that for reasons that I'll explain later.

You also need to find a venture that doesn't require a tremendous amount of technical expertise. And you need some software such as a text editor or word processor and an image editor. There is even freeware (free computer software) that can be downloaded for these purposes. Moreover, you want something that doesn't require much software expertise and certainly not a degree in computer programming. In addition, you need something that doesn't take too long on a daily basis.

Just as in my eBay research, you need to find a source of a product to sell. We've already narrowed the products to those of an adult nature. Fortunately, there are many sources of these adult products so this will be easier than for eBay.

Finally, you need to find a way to connect your product to the money. This will probably be though billing sites as were mentioned in an earlier chapter. eBay would never have been successful if its founders had not found a way for sellers to collect money on the Internet. So eBay used PayPal as its principal money collection and payment arm. In fact, eBay now owns PayPal. However, eBay and PayPal have do not want to become involved in porn. So you will need to user other billing companies that specialize in the adult Internet. Let's look at the pros and cons of some types of adult sites:

Pay Sites

These sites are pretty much the Cadillac of the industry. They feature tens of thousands of high quality photos and videos. Most of these sites operate on a membership basis where the purchaser pays with a credit card for a monthly membership. Usually, these renew automatically unless the customer fills out a cancellation request. This keeps the money flowing into the site as many guys simply forget to cancel or sometimes are too embarrassed to call an 800 number for customer service. The typical site costs $30-40 per month, and the average customer stays four months. The big pay sites have thousands of members at any one time. They are usually updated daily or at least once a week and may have full-time employees. Many pay sites are part of a larger network that many have a dozen or more sites operating at once.

While there's big money in pay sites, there're also big expenses. These sites require a huge amount of bandwidth for their server operations. They also use expensive dedicated servers that handle only their own site traffic. They have professional programmers and pay commissions to other adult webmasters for forwarding traffic to their sites. You need a lot of experience to start a pay site. You also need a lot of capital. It has been estimated that the money required to start and operate a first-class pay site for the first year in today's market is about $500,000. Oops! That leaves us out.

Dating Sites

Dating sites can be general interest sites or adult oriented sites. While such sites are intended mainly for adults, the adult oriented versions contain much more sexually graphic content. These function somewhat like pay sites in that they sell monthly memberships. The problem with creating such a site is that you must have a large group of members to be successful. And, how do you build your membership? This is not like a traditional pay site where you can buy content from brokers. It is really difficult to build up an active dating site that will produce income. Check out the following which is one of the top adult dating sites:

Adult Friend Finder

http://www.adultfriendfinder.com/

Adult Toys, Novelties, and DVD Sites

Go visit a big adult bookstore. You'll find all kinds of vibrators, dildos, lingerie, and novelty items on the shelves. Obviously, there is a demand for this stuff, or the stores wouldn't stock it. Now imagine selling the same products online. First, you'll have to find a wholesale source of products and stock an inventory. Your website won't have to be extremely large because you can easily get a dozen or more products on each page with pages categorized by type of product. On the other hand, a DVD site might be huge due to the large number of new DVDs coming out each month. And the inventory will quickly fill your garage or basement. While vibrators and dildos don't change much from month to month, DVD titles are quick going out of date with the demand always being for the newest titles. Yuck!

The adult products website becomes less attractive when you consider the additional chores of packing and shipping along with collecting sales tax and reporting to you state's tax bureau. In addition, there are laws against selling adult products in some states. These laws have been enforced in recent court decisions. Another problem is that it's difficult to obtain a credit card billing system for these types of sites. Most banks are just not interested in issuing merchant accounts for online merchandise sales.

Surprisingly enough, eBay offers an adult category that most people don't know about. Go to the eBay homepage and click on the Categories link. You should see a drop-down box. Click on "Everything Else" which is the last item. Then click on "Mature

Audiences". You'll find about 60,000 adult oriented items including toys, homemade DVDs, books, CDs, clothing, and trading cards. As you browse through these items, note that PayPal does not allow using its payment method in the Mature Audiences section. (There are some alternative billing systems that do handle adult products sales.)

If you're really set on selling adult merchandise, your best bet might be to go with eBay where you'll have a built-in audience of users who are seeking such products. And, there's a lot of variety in the merchandise you can offer. However, eBay sales are beyond the realm of this book. eBay offers excellent support for new sellers, and there are dozens of books available at your bookstore or online.

Link Sites

These sites feature pages of links to other sites. One of the most famous is *Persian Kitty* (http://www.persiankitty.com) although there are many others. The most successful sites are those that got started back in the nineties. The idea is that adult webmasters submit link requests using a form provided by the link site. Each request is for a specific adult site on the requestor's web server. The sites are usually small free sites with two to four galleries of nude pictures or several videos. Link sites are always free to use and are a great source of free porn. The link site makes its money with banner ads on its pages. Some link sites even sell advertising space. A submitted link is usually left on the link site for at least several weeks.

To be successful with a link site you will need to make contact with hundreds of webmasters to get submissions for you links. Problems arise because you're pretty much at the mercy of these other webmasters who are really unknown to you. What happens if a guy submits an innocent enough looking gallery that leads to a site containing child porn or a computer virus? You'll be in big trouble fast. Another problem is with webmasters who submit a decent looking page to you, and then modify the page after it's been approved. If you're getting a large number of submissions, just reviewing them for the approval process can take hours each day. Managing a link site can take a lot of time so that really doesn't fit our stated criteria. Some of the top link sites include the following:

Greenguy's Link-O-Rama
http://www.link-o-rama.com/

Persian Kitty
http://www.persiankitty.com/

Richard's Realm
http://www.richardsrealm.com/

Thumbnail Gallery Post Site (TGP)

     TGPs have been one of the hottest areas for adult webmasters. It is essentially similar to a link site except that the submitted links connect directly to single page galleries rather than complete websites. These pages usually contain about sixteen thumbnail pictures of a naked girl plus a couple of banner advertisements for adult pay sites. The viewer clicks on a thumb to see the full size photo. This is another great source for free porn. One of the most popular is *The Hun's Yellow Pages* (http://www.thehun.com). A listing usually stays on the TGP site for only a few days as they have a constant source of new submissions each day.

     The problems with these sites are similar to those for link lists. A popular TGP site uses a tremendous amount of bandwidth. Some hosting companies cannot handle this type of server traffic and prohibit TGP pages. A listing on The Hun might get well over 10,000 hits a day. If your site is not hosted on a heavy duty server, such a listing may bring down the whole server, and your hosting account may get cancelled quickly.

     In addition, if you're giving away too much free porn, how can you expect to make money? Most of the users who frequent TGPs and link sites are looking for free porn. They are freeloaders - not potential buyers. Many TGP viewers are in parts of the world where credit cards are not commonly used. Serving up thousands of free images to people who are not potential buyers is a total waste of your efforts. While there is money to be made in TGP sites, they are not for beginners.

That said, we may use TGPs as part of our business plan. We will use them by submitting our own galleries to TGP sites. In addition, we will submit our own websites to link lists. How this is done will be discussed later. Following are some major TGP sites to peruse. Note that you'll have to skip way down on the page past all the ads to find the actual daily listings submitted by other webmasters.

The Hun
http://www.thehun.net/

Thumbzilla
http://www.thumbzilla.com

The New Shemp
http://www.shemp.com

Free Site

This is usually a small site the may consist of only a few pages. It starts with a Warning Page followed by the Main Page. There are 2-4 links on the Main Page that lead to galleries of thumbnails for individual girls. Each gallery is similar to a TGP page. So the surfer gets a free look at several sets of naked girl photos. In keeping with admonition above, we don't want to provide too much free stuff. The photos and text of the site should be a come-hither to entice the surfer to join a porn site. The galleries for example may be from a single pay site along with text that entices the surfer to believe that he can find more of the same by joining. On every page are several advertising banners or text links leading to the sponsors pay site. The free site earns its income through commissions paid by the pay site for each new signup.

Thus, the free site is really and advertising tool, and your purpose as a webmaster is to direct your visitors to the paid product. This is not unlike a billboard advertising business except that they don't have the naked girls. What you get paid is a commission that depends upon the specific programs offered by the pay site sponsors. The commission arrangements will be covered in a later chapter.

Free sites are placed on your web server and usually left for a long time. In fact, you may never take them down as long as they are getting hits (traffic) and the sponsors are still paying. Each free site is on its own subdirectory in your hosted website area. Some webmasters create a new free site several times a week. Their idea is that if one free site generates some income, surely a hundred sites will do better. This is unlike a TGP page where the page is submitted to a TGP submission site and only appears for a few days before it is superseded by newer pages.

The free site concept is in keeping with our desire to find a product that doesn't require a lot of time. Once you've created a few free sites, the others are often carbon copies with similar templates but different gallery photos. You can get traffic for you site by submitting it to link sites like *Persian Kitty*. It can also be submitted to the various search engines. The text of your pages can be carefully crafted to get high rankings on searches. For example, a high ranking for a particular set of search terms like "sexy girls" can get hundreds of hits a day from sites like Google and Yahoo. In addition, the gallery pages you create can be modified slightly and submitted to TGP sites for more traffic.

It is important to remember that the purpose of a free site is to make money. For that you'll need to convince them to buy memberships in the pay sites you are promoting. You will give away some free porn to attract the surfer. Giving away too much for free defeats your purpose. Keep a limit on the free stuff and don't display hardcore. Always tease the surfer that there's more better stuff at the pay site.

For examples of free sites, go to any of the link list sites mentioned above and click through the listings. Again, you'll have to skip half way down on the page past all the banner ads to find the lists.

Turnkey Site

In all the above discussion, it is assumed that you will be creating your own site, no matter which type it is. There is also the possibility of purchasing a turnkey website that has been totally constructed and developed by another company. This company usually provides a package of services including the hosting on its own server. These sites are marketed as a way for the beginning webmaster to quickly take advantage of the income producing potential of porn with little effort or knowledge. You pay for the initial package plus a monthly hosting fee.

There are some advantages and a lot of disadvantages to turnkey operations. The provider offers quality graphics, design, and layout. It also provides all the content. You may be able to include your own choice of sponsors but in many cases all sponsor links go to pay site programs run by the provider. For the most part you don't have much control of your site. You will probably not be able to change your Meta Tags or optimize your pages for search engine traffic. And you still have to promote your site. There are a few turnkey providers who will essentially program an entire site and turn the code and contents over to you. These are essentially offering one time programming services. To me, these are preferable to the package turnkey offerings.

The real problem with turnkey programs is they may cost thousands of dollars as a startup expense. And they may be selling the same site design and contents over and over. In addition, you don't learn much about webmastering in the process so you're still in the dark about how to make money. For these reasons I don't recommend turnkey programs.

Conclusion

This chapter has described six types of adult sites that can make money. Of these, the free site is the only model that can easily be learned by a beginning webmaster. Therefore, we will design a model for making money with free sites in a future chapter. Note that the basic design is a template that can be varied in many ways not only as to site design, but as to photo content and sponsored ads. To create your first site you will need a few tools: a text editor, a graphics editor, and a file transfer program (FTP) to move your files to a web server. These tools can be obtained very cheaply or even as free downloads from various websites. You don't need a lot of technical knowledge about how to use these programs. You will also need a bit of knowledge about how to write code for your web pages in the hypertext markup language (HTML). That is totally beyond the scope of this document. There are literally hundreds of books available on HTML coding. The "...for Dummies" books and SAMS "Teach Yourself..." series are an excellent place to start. The following chapters will present the basic outline of how to start designing a site. Finally, you're going to need some content (pictures), and you'll find a chapter on where to locate good inexpensive photos.

General vs. Niche Content

When I started my first porn site, I had grandiose ideas for how it would develop. At first it was a free site with about forty pictures spread through five galleries on a general "babes" theme. That is to say hot women ranging from teens up to their late twenties. Somehow I imagined that as this site grew it would encompass more and more genres of porn much like a large pay site. For instance: tits, asses, teens, babes, amateurs, hardcore, and even celebrities. I soon learned that it is better to focus on one specific area rather than create sites that are too general in there appeal. Thus, most of my sites became teen or college-girl oriented. It certainly didn't hurt that teens were one of the hottest genres and still are. Of course, teens can only refer to those girls over eighteen for legal reasons. So there has been a tendency to substitute the term "young ladies" as a generic identifier for the 18-19 year-old girls.

The content categories mentioned above are some of the most popular for pay sites. It is natural, then, that if you create sites along these lines, you will be able to feed your surfers to the appropriate pay sites.

There's also money to be made in niche sites meaning a specialized market that doesn't fit into these basic categories. They are more geared to customers looking for specialized areas which are sometimes labeled as fetish content. A niche site offers more unique content which won't compete with the big pay sites. There are niche sponsors who offer affiliate programs to which you can direct this specialized traffic.

There are many niche areas, and they correspond to various offbeat and unusual sexual desires. Some of these niche subjects are really a turnoff for most webmasters such as scat (poop) or hard bondage. The secret of running a successful niche is to choose only a subject that you are comfortable with. Don't run a gay site, for example, unless you're comfortable with that life style. Also bear in mind that you can't market these sites to the general adult public. They have limited appeal that you'll have to seek out in your search for web traffic. The big advantage is that those who are seeking niche material will recognize the value of your site and are more like to lay out some bucks to get more of it. Thus, obscure sexual impulses can lead to money in your pocket even though your customer base is much smaller. On the next page is a listing of some of the major niche areas in no particular order. You can find pay site sponsors to match any of these.

Niches

- Blow Jobs
- Big Tits
- Asses and Anal Sex
- Upskirts
- Foot Fetishes
- Bondage and Sado-masochism (BDSM)
- Mature
- Interracial
- Pregnant
- Ebony
- Gay
- Hair Colors (redheads, blondes, brunettes)
- Pantyhose and Stockings
- Asian
- Shaved Girls
- Hairy Girls
- Softcore Glamour
- Big Beautiful Women (BBW)
- Mothers I Like To Fuck (MILF)
- Voyeurism
- Transsexuals
- Exhibitionism / Outdoors
- Party Girls
- Monster Cocks
- Group Sex
- Latino/Hispanic
- Smoking
- Porn Stars
- Celebrities

Tattoos and Piercing
Imprisonment
Bisexual
Lesbian
Creampie
Lingerie
Masturbation
Shemale
Female Squirting
Webcams
Vintage Porn

Sponsor/Affiliate Programs

The essence of our money making plan is to become affiliated with pay sites that will pay a commission for each new customer that we bring to them. These pay sites are called "sponsors" and each individual webmaster sending traffic is an "affiliate". Becoming an affiliate is easy and costs nothing. On the warning page or main page of each pay site, there is usually a small link at the bottom marked "Webmasters". This will take you to the affiliate signup area. Most pay sites will have a couple of programs based on different models. The two most popular are explained below:

Pay-Per-Signup

With these programs the affiliate gets a fixed payment for each new signup. The amounts are not trivial and are sometimes on a graduated scale depending upon the total number of signups set per month. For example:

1-50 signups	Pays $30 per signup
51-100	Pays $35 per signup
101 or more	Pays $40 per signup

As you can see the affiliate webmaster is rewarded for the more traffic and signups he can generate. Payments are usually issued every two weeks or monthly in the form of a check mailed to the affiliate. Many programs also provide for wire transfer of large amounts which is most useful to foreign webmasters. There is usually a minimum payment amount per pay period such as $50. This means that if the amount you earned in a particular pay period is less that the minimum, your money will be held until such time as the aggregate of your earnings exceeds the minimum. Then a payment will be issued. As you look at sponsor programs, be sure to check the fine print in the terms and conditions which usually contains the payment details. Also check the frequently asked questions section in the signup area for additional clarification.

With pay-per-signup you only get paid for the original membership signup. These are usually recurring memberships and the pay site gets to keep all the income from renewals. That's really how they make their money. Many sites have a monthly membership fee of around $30 so if they pay you the first month, then they don't make anything to cover their other expenses until the ensuing months. So why can't you just sign up yourself and for the first month knowing you'll earn your money back in a commission. You can usually do that without problem. Just be sure to cancel before the end of the month. If you're going to be promoting a site, it's usually a good idea to join the site so you can see just exactly what it offers and what is the quality of the product. This can also help in developing an advertising strategy.

Many pay sites are part of a larger group of sites that all fall under the same sponsor program. These may be sites that are similar in content and emphasis such as a group of teen girl and young women sites or they may run the gamut of adult niches and even fetishes. It is not unusual for a sponsor program to have as many as two dozen sites to promote.

Recurring Payment Programs

These programs are based on the concept that the affiliate webmaster is more of a continuing partner with the sponsor. There is an agreed percentage split of the income from memberships as 50/50 or 60/40. The first value is the percentage the affiliate gets on the signup and each renewal. The second is the amount the sponsor keeps. So let's assume that a membership signup costs $30 per month. On a 50/50 split program, you would be $15 each month and the sponsor keeps $15. While you get paid less at first than with the pay-per-signup, the monthly renewals can add up to considerably more. This can go on even for years. I have one fellow who signed up for a teen site several years ago and has never cancelled. So each month, his credit card gets billed for another $30 and I get a payment for half of that. In some instances, I think the members do not accurately monitor their credit card bills and have no idea that they're still paying. There's nothing wrong with that, and I'm more than happy to receive my commission.

Some sponsors offer only recurring payment programs as they feel that the commission split is a better business model and less subject to abuse.

Adult Verification Systems

AVS systems earn their money by serving as a doorway offering access to a large number of porn sites. In essence they "verify" that the surfer is an adult of legal age by requiring a credit card purchase of a membership fee. The website earns its money as a partial commission from the membership fee. This is used to legally protect the adult website from penalties for distributing objectionable content. AVS systems were common back in the 1990's, but there aren't too many still around. Webmasters who have small sites of niche content sometimes use the AVS model as a way to collect money. The surfer buys a membership giving access to the hole group of AVS sites (which may be hundreds of sites) instead to buy directly into the desired site. Some of the more popular AVS systems include:

Cyberage

http://www.cyberage.com

Sexkey

http://www.sexkey.com

Adult Bouncer

http://www.adultbouncer.com

Pay Per Click

These sponsors pay you a few cents for each click you send. There are a lot of rules so it's not as easy as click and pay. Each webmaster is assigned an affiliate ID just like other types of programs. When the surfer clicks on a banner or text link, the sponsor tracks that activity. This takes the surfer to the first page of the sponsor's site. Nobody pays anymore for first page clicks because too many times the surfer just hits the back button. When the surfer clicks deeper into the site, that is called a "second page hit", and that will pay. What happens if the surfer clicks these pages more than once? Do you get paid each time? No way. Hits are counted only if they are unique meaning only the first hit gets counted. Further, if your unique hits do not result in enough membership sales, the sponsor generally reserves the right to convert you to a pay per signup program only. The pay per click model is gradually falling by the wayside because it is too subject to fraud.

Email and Password Programs

These sponsors collect email addresses by offering a number of free goodies. In return for his email address, the surfer gets free porn in his email box daily or free passwords to porn sites. The sponsor is able to gather a large collection of valid email addresses of persons who are interested in porn. The sponsor can now offer the surfer other pay sites. This is called "upselling." The sponsor can also simply market the email addresses to other sponsors. The affiliate webmaster gets a small payment ($1.00-$1.50) per email address garnered. Not a fortune but the secret here is quantity.

These programs are not hard to market since they appear to be offering something that seems free to the surfer in return for his email address. Can't you just submit a bunch of email addresses of your friends (or enemies)? No way because all these sponsors go through a verification process before considering the submitted address to be valid. First, they send an email to the address advising the recipient about the nature of the site offered. He must confirm his membership by clicking a validation link. Only verified memberships result in payments to the affiliate.

Email/password programs offer a variety of banners and text links for promotion just like the major pay sites. In fact, they are often offshoots of the big sites. These are ideal links to stick at the bottom of a web page to catch a surfer who hasn't clicked on anything else. One of the sites I have used with success:

Teen-Mail4Free

http://www.teen-mail4free.com/

Caution - don't sign up for this site unless you really want a lot of porn in your mail box. Click on the link marked "Webmasters" at the bottom of the signup page, and it'll take you to the sponsor's webmaster area for *CECash*.

Shaving Hits

Each time one of your surfers clicks on a link on one of your sites, he is taken to one of your affiliated sponsors. That is called a hit. So, if one hundred of your surfers click on a link for Sponsor X on a certain day, you would expect to log into the sponsor's affiliate statistics area and find one hundred hits recorded for the day. Often, this is true. In fact, most of the time a sponsors stats will show fewer hits that you actually sent. If the sponsor is deliberately under reporting your clicks, that is called "shaving hits." It may be a sign of a less than reputable sponsor, and you'll find guys complaining about this all the time on the message boards. Whether this is actually due to deliberate shaving or some other idiosyncrasy of the click-through process is hard to determine. I would not be overly concerned about under-reported clicks. Most major sponsors are honest, and those that use third party click processors such as CCBill will have a hard time cheating you.

Signing Up with Sponsors

When I find a pay site that I personally like, I look for the "Webmasters" link that is usually near the bottom of one of the first pages. The first thing I look for is the list of sites that fall under that sponsor. These usually have banners or text links that will take you to the individual sites. Look them over with a mind to how you can promote those sites and how they will fit into your scheme of what you want to do. For example, let's assume you're going to create a free teen girls website. You will want to look for sponsor sites that fit into that genre such as teens or twenty-something young ladies. You will not need mature ladies sites, gay sites, or bondage sites for your match since you will want to match your surfers to the type of content they're viewing.

Next, look for promotional materials provided by the sponsor. These are usually banners, text links, small videos, picture sets, and hosted galleries. Here I'm looking for the quality and quantity of the offerings. These promotional materials are always free. Banners are particularly important because you're going to put a number of them on your websites. They usually come in some standard sizes described as 468 x 60, 468 x 80 and larger. The first value is the pixel size of the width and the second value is the height so these would be horizontal banners. Vertical banners would have sizes such as 80 x 400. Samples of the banners are always displayed on the pages so you can see how large they are in relationship to your monitor screen.

Most sponsors now offer free hosted galleries (FHG). These are ready made thumbnail galleries that at hosted on the sponsor's servers. The sponsor will give you the links (URLs) to a variety of galleries designed for the pay site you wish to advertise. The way this works is that each affiliate has a special login ID or code assigned. This ID needs to be included in the link provided by the sponsor. You may need to add the ID manually with a text editor or many sponsors automatically generate the ID as part of the linking code provided. So you put the link on your webpage with text link "Hot & Sexy Girls Getting Naked" or a thumbnail image extracted from the gallery. Clicking your link will automatically take the surfer to the sponsor's server and display the gallery. If the surfer purchases a membership from the gallery, your ID will be passed on into the sponsor's database, and you will get credit for the sale. The advantages of the free hosted galleries are that they are professionally prepared and you have no bandwidth cost to display them. A disadvantage is that lots of guys use the same galleries so you don't have original content on your site. Also, if you submit your site to link lists and TGPs, those webmasters have seen all the hosted galleries many times and will reject your submission.

If the sponsor passes my test for appropriate promotional content, I will next read the terms and conditions. This is a legally binding contract. Most of the contracts are similar. I look for things like where is the sponsor located. Since I am a United States webmaster, I want only sponsors located in the U.S. or who use U.S. billing companies. Another thing to look for is who will handle the commission payments. Some sponsors do their own commission processing. Many use third party billing companies. In most cases I'd rather deal with a third party company because they are independent of the sponsor and have their own reputation to protect. The way this works is that the monthly membership payments are paid directly to the third party processor via credit card. The processor then splits the payment between the sponsor and the affiliate webmaster. So the sponsor never gets its hands on your portion of the money.

Also check for a frequently asked questions (FAQ) page which often covers most webmaster concerns. Be sure you understand how the payments will be made and how often, and especially be aware of any minimum balances required before you issuing a check.

Ready to sign up? There are a couple of other issues to consider. Click the link for the signup form where you will find a number of standard items:

- Name & mailing address
- Your age - must be at least 18 to enter into a contract
- Email address
- Type of program - there may be several options
- URL of your website
- Social Security Number

The last two present problems: Sponsors usually want to see the URL of an adult website that you are running. Therefore, you need to create your first site along the lines explained later so the sponsor can see the site even though it will have no banners at that point. The sponsor wants to know that your site is presentable and ready to go. This requirement also prevents guys who are not really adult webmasters from just signing up to get access to the free galleries.

Social security numbers are generally required from U.S. webmasters because the IRS requires that the sponsor report your commissions (if over $600 a year) on Form 1099. Yes, Virginia, you do have to pay taxes on your earnings. I shutter when I think how many times I gave out my SSN in the early years to sponsor programs that I really didn't know a thing about. When you operate without a company, you are classified as a sole proprietor. Supplying the SSN for tax purposes is just one of the costs of getting started even though we live in an age where identity theft is common. I have never had any reason to believe that any sponsor used my SSN in an inappropriate way. Still, there is a way around this problem. You can apply to the IRS for an employer identification number (EIN). This is a nine-digit number that looks just like a SSN, but it will be used for your company dealings such as employee payroll. EINs are free, and you get obtain one online from the official government website at this URL:

Internal Revenue Service EIN Information
http://www.irs.gov/businesses/small/article/0,,id=98350,00.html

Basically, the IRS only wants to issue EINs to entities who will have employees so that's one of the questions you will be asked. Just assume that you'll have some employees in the future. You might answer that you expect to employ five persons, and that's certainly not out of line if your business grows. You will receive your new EIN immediately after submitting the application. Be sure to print the page and keep the number in a safe place. Now use the EIN in place of your SSN on any sponsorship applications.

After you submit your signup form to the sponsor, you should receive an immediate response via the web. This will contain your sponsor ID number and directions for logging into their affiliate's website area where you will find the promotional materials, links, and other goodies. You'll also probably get a response by email. Be sure to print out all these items. I made up a loose-leaf notebook titled "Sponsors" to hold all this partnership material.

Locating Content

Content is the heart of your site. Adult content consists of photos, videos, and sometimes stories. (We won't deal with stories here although you can find people who make a living writing adult fiction.) When I started out in the nineties, the biggest question was where to get professional quality photos of naked girls. Using search engines, I found numerous photographers mostly located in large cities who offered CD collections of their own nude photo shoots. Prices were high - $100 to $200 for a CD with about six girls in 30-40 poses for each shoot. Fortunately, prices have come down over the years, and you no longer have to wait for the CD to arrive in the mail because content can be downloaded in a matter of minutes.

Downloadable content is usually sold by the set rather than a whole CD-full. You pick out the girl you want and usually see a screen full of thumbnails of photos from the set. With the set come the full-sized images and often the corresponding thumbnails. Don't be too concerned about getting the thumbs because we assume you'll be using your image editing program to create thumbs of the appropriate size for your site. By editing your own thumbs, you can also compress the images so they load super fast. And you can tightly crop them down to just the most important parts of the image. Thumbs don't have to display the entire image. A thumb should be enough to coax your viewer to click it to see more. In some instances you may not even want to show full nudity in the thumb. For example, you might just show the model's head shot with an enticing "click here to see more of me" text link. Most photo sets have 30-60 images - many of which are near duplicates. You know, the kind of thing where the model moves slightly from image to image. In any photo set, examine the thumbnail previews carefully to determine if you'll be able to extract enough different poses to make a complete gallery. A single gallery might have 10 to 16 images. Most TGP sites and link list sites require a minimum of ten images per gallery. Let's talk about different sources of content:

Paid Content

Content is sold by individual photographers who produce their own images and by content brokers who offer the work of many photo studios. Many of the good sources of content are located in Europe particularly around Prague and Budapest. These studios offer beautiful girls and top notch photography on interesting sets or backgrounds. Gone are the days when a photographer just took a girl out in the woods are to a hotel to shoot pics. Some of the top notch studios feature lavish sets that are also used for full length porn video shoots. Unlike hosting, content is one area where I do not feel there is any problem in dealing with brokers out of your country. Some of the major European brokers even operated their websites using dedicated servers located in the United States. You may be able to determine this by running a whois search on their site URL.

One of the problems for beginning adult webmasters is that you may be asked to register on a content site before being given access to the samples. You may be asked for the name of your adult site URL. In most cases I don't think they actually check out your site since the registration seems instantaneous. However, it does seem that you need to have purchased a URL and set up a hosting account somewhere with at least an "under construction" page. Another way around this problem is to set up your site using free content that is provided by you sponsors. That at least give you a sample site to help prove you're a legitimate adult webmaster.

My suggestion is to signup with a couple of paid content providers and purchase a small amount of downloadable photo sets. Purchases are usually paid by credit card and downloads are available as soon as your card is approved. This whole transaction usually takes just a couple of minutes. In some instances the provider has to actually assemble the content for your download which may take a couple of hours to a day. You'll get back an email with the exact URL location of the download and instructions. Remember that content brokers aren't at work in the middle of the night. If you're located in New Jersey and the content broker is in Prague, there's a six hour time difference. So if you order later in the day, the folks in

Prague may already have gone home for the day. Order early in the day or just be patient. In general you can't use PayPal to purchase adult content because PayPal doesn't want that kind of business.

One provider of cheap adult content that I recommend is the *Paul Markham Content Store*. Paul is a Czech photographer located in Prague who's been in business for years. He has two sites that complement each other: *paulmarkham.com* and *bargainbasementcontent.com*.

At the first site, Paul offers downloads of his most recent work featuring gorgeous Czech girls mainly in the teen and babe genre. Most of those sets cost about $40 for around 100 photos. These can be downloaded by FTP. You place your order on the web. Paul and his wife, Eva, assemble your sets and send an email with the exact location of the content. Then you use FTP to retrieve your purchase. Sets include large photos, thumbnails, and 2257 info on each model purchases. Paul also offers video clips of many of his models.

The second bargain site is similar only the sets are older having originally appeared on the first site. The most amazing thing is that most of the bargain sets cost $5-10. There's no tax and no shipping charges since delivery is via FTP. You can browse both these sites for free. You need to create a login ID if you want to be able to view the larger sample photos. These sites are a good starting place for the beginning webmaster who wants to keep down his content costs:

Paul Markham Content
http://www.paulmarkham.com/

Bargain Basement Content
http://www.bargainbasementcontent.com/

Other sites offering reasonably priced content are as follows:

Amateur Cutie Content

http://www.amateur-cutie-content.com/

Web Legal Content
http://www.web-legal.com/

Adult Content (CA)
http://www.adultcontent.ca/

Adult Content (UK)
http://www.adultcontent.co.uk/

Adult Czech Content
http://www.adultczechcontent.com/

Do-It-Yourself Content

     If you ask a number of guys why they go into the porn business, you'll always find a few who had grandiose ideas about setting up their own studio where they could photograph beautiful naked women. You could start by photographing your own wife or girl friend but that's kind of limited. You also need cameras, lights, and a location. There're only so many shots you can shoot in your living room or bedroom. If you're located in a big city or college town, you may be able to locate models by advertising in the classified section of papers. These models don't read the *New York Times* so you'll need to locate underground or advertising tabloids. These often carry ads for adult bookstores and the like. Place discreet ads and make it clear that nudity is involved. Something like this: "Photographer needs college girl types for nude modeling. Good pay." If you get phone calls, make it clear that no sex is involved. Otherwise, the local vice squad will be looking you up.

     If you have a wife or girl friend, it may be a good idea to have her take the calls from prospective models to assure them you're shoots are on the up-and-up. Strip clubs in your town might also be a good place to locate models. After all, these girls are already used to taking off the clothes. Just be discrete in your inquiries. If you make contact with some potential models over the phone, don't just invite them to your studio. Ask them to send or email a couple of photos (head shot and full body clothed or bikini shot). This will save you a lot of misery.

Shooting your own content is an awful lot of work, and I really don't recommend it. If your real goal is to meet girls and see some skin, do it some other way. It'll be a lot cheaper and will keep you out of trouble.

Free Sponsor Content

What could be better than free? Most sponsors offer photo galleries and short videos of their models without charge. After you register with the sponsor, you should receive an email with information about their affiliate web site that contains links, banners, and content. Some sponsors have hundreds of galleries of free content.

Sponsor's content is often assembled into zipped files (compressed files) that you download. After uncompressing, you'll probably find a lot of very similar poses. Your job is to find about sixteen interesting poses of each girl that can be assembled into your gallery. If there isn't much variety in the shots, you may be able to use your image editor to create two photos by cropping one image in tight and using the full image as a second photo. For instance, one shot is a full frontal shot and the second is a tightly cropped shot of the model's face and boobs. Two for one! Sometimes, I've had to do that but not too often.

Another type of sponsor content is the Free Hosted Gallery (FHG). These have become extremely popular in the last few years. The FHG consists of a number of pictures arranged into a professionally created gallery. And the gallery is on the sponsor's server so you have no bandwidth charges. You simply link with the sponsor provided URL that is customized to include your affiliate ID. If the surfer joins a site while viewing the FHG, you get your percentage of the commission. This is incredibly easy. In fact, your free site could consist of a just a couple of web pages that contain links to several FHG pages. While the FHG seems to be the beginning adult webmaster's dream solution, read on to learn what's wrong with them.

The big problem with sponsor content and FHG's is that every one of their affiliates is using the same stuff. That means your site is not unique. When the sponsor puts out new galleries from time to time, everyone incorporates those new photos into his sites. Some of your big traffic-getters come from TGP and link list submissions. Unfortunately, everybody submits his new galleries to those sites. The TGP and link list webmasters are sick of seeing the same old content over and over. They'll reject your gallery in an instant if they recognize the photos.

Also, if you're primarily using sponsor content, why shouldn't the owner of the TGP or link list just sign up with the sponsor directly and receive all the membership commissions himself? This is a problem that has arisen with the rise in popularity of hosted galleries. As sponsors are providing more and more free content, the list webmasters are no longer so dependent upon gallery submissions from other webmasters. They can just link directly to the sponsor's content like any other webmaster and reap the profits therewith. This has caused some list webmasters to limit the number of outside submissions they accept. This is why you need unique content, and you're more likely to find that by purchasing from content brokers and photographers.

Stolen Content

Finally we address something that happens all too often. With so many free sites on the web, why not just go out there and pick some galleries you like and steal the content. Or join your favorite pay site for a month and steal away a ton of its content. It's certainly easy - just right-click on the image and select the option to save it to your computer. This is obviously wrong in both a legal and moral sense. The images you take may be secretly embedded with watermarks that identify their source. Pay site images often have logos or other identifying marks in the corner of the photo. In addition, there are copyright issues that may get you sued. The worst possibility of all is to have stolen images of a model who is under eighteen years of age and to wind up with a child pornography charge. This book is

41

premised on the assumption that you want to establish a legal money-making business so don't start by taking other people's work.

Domain Names

A first hurdle for the budding adult webmaster is to purchase a domain name for your site. This involves searching for a name that is not already taken and purchasing the domain for a period of one or more years. Domains can be purchased from any number of domain name registrars. All registrars have the same names available. For example, suppose you find that "veryhotgirls.com" is available. You can purchase the right to use that domain through any of the registrars. Surprisingly, the price may vary anywhere from $15-$35 for a single year. A lot depends on what services the registrar provides with the domain so shop around. The last part of the domain name (after the period) is called the extension such as .com, .net, .us, .info, etc. By far, the .com domains are the most popular the hardest to find. They are also considered to be more valuable if you later want to sell your domain. My advice is to try for a .com domain.

There are two approaches to domain names for your sites. The first is to buy a separate name for each site you operate. This is difficult because most of the good names are taken. It will also cost you an annual fee for every site. The advantage is that the names, when available, can be very specific in describing the content of your site. A name such as "veryhotgirls.com" suggests what your site is all about.

The second approach is to purchase one generic sounding domain name that will house all your sites. Each site will then be on a subdirectory of the main name. The main name does not have to sound like and adult site at all. In fact you may also locate other non-adult money making sites on the same domain. The domain name could sound like a hosting company even though you will not be running a web hosting business. For example, I once registered the name "teenhosts.com". On that one domain I had a number of teen oriented websites - each with its own subdirectory:

teenhosts.com/teeniemax	TeenieMax site
teenhosts.com/hotgirls	Hot Girls site
teenhosts.com/realteengirls	Real Teen Girls site

Using this method you only pay to renew one URL each year, and it gives you a lot more flexibility. To create a new website I just create a new subdirectory and get started. It's also much easier to find a generic-sounding domain name than to find the adult specific names.

Finding a good domain name is not easy. Fortunately, there are a number of good websites to help. All active domain names are contained in databases operated by the Internet Corporation for Assigned Numbers and Numbers (ICANN). With each name is information that was entered by the purchaser such as address, phone number and email address of the registrant, administrator, and technical contact. In addition, ICANN has set up contracts with companies around the world that serve as Domain Name Registrars. At each registrar's website you will find a "whois" program that will query the ICANN data and display the registration information about each site. In the nineties all domain registrations were handled by Network Solutions. Their whois program is located at this URL:

Network Solutions Whois

http://www.networksolutions.com/en_US/whois/index.jhtml

Other examples of registrar's whois pages are shown below:

DirectNic Whois

http://www.directnic.com/whois/

GoDaddy Whois

http://who.godaddy.com/whoischeck.aspx

Try looking up this site in a whois program: Enter a URL like "cnn.com" and click the search button. You'll see all the whois data. Moreover, the existence of this data means this name is taken. (The whois info also shows when the domain registration will expire.) Try modifying the URL in the search box to something that doesn't exist such as "xxxcnnxxx.com". You'll find the domain is not in use so you could purchase it. Often the whois program will display a button that takes you directly to one of the domain registrar's signup page where you can complete the purchase. Just be aware that once you find an available domain, you don't have to purchase it from a specific registrar. Any ICANN registrar can handle the purchase transaction and prices do differ. There are also many independently operated whois programs such as:

Psychic Whois

http://www.psychicwhois.com/

Better Whois

http://www.betterwhois.com/

Who.Is

http://www.whois.ws/

Another method of finding an available name is to go to the main page of any of the registrars and use their domain search box. This is different from the whois function in that it doesn't return information about an existing domain. It just tells you whether a name is in use. If taken, the programs will usually suggest other similar names that are available. For example, if you search for "veryhotgirls.com", the program may tell you the domain is already taken, and it may suggest an alternate that is still available with a different extension such as "veryhotgirls.info".

Hint: when you search for a domain name, always leave out the "www" and "http://." So enter in the box "veryhotgirls.com" (no quotes) - not "www.veryhotgirls.com."

So now you first task is cut out for you: to find an available domain name. If you choose to go with a specific adult sounding name, your task will be very difficult because most everything is taken. All two, three, and four letter .com domains are already taken like aaa.com, aab.com, aac.com, etc. so don't waste your time. A generic sounding name will be easier. Because so many domains are already taken, it is usually easier to build up a potential name by combining three words. Let's start with "girls." There's no use searching for "girls.com" or any variation. Try if you like. Now let's add an adjective that further describes our domain. Here are some possibilities:

    hotgirls.com
    sexygirls.com
    xxxgirls.com

Notice that I have combined the words into a single word. This is usually the preferred naming method. However, you may also separate words with a hyphen such as hot-girls.com, sexy-girls.com, etc. Some webmasters prefer the hyphenated names because they thing that search engines will rank them higher. (The jury is still out on this.) You probably won't find any of these name combinations to be available so we need to add another adjective to create a three word combination:

    veryhotgirls.com
    mysexygirls.com
    dirtyteengirls.com

A three-word-combination is more likely to be available. Just keep each word short in length. You want something simple for your domain name - not a tongue twister. It is important that the surfer be able to remember your domain name and type it into the browser without errors.

If you choose to go with a generic name, follow the same principles. Also, consider phonetic equivalents. Since "cyberhosting.com" is probably taken, try "syberhosting.com".

There is also a legal issue to consider in choosing a name. Registering a domain name that is very similar to a large corporation is risky because you may run afoul of trademark law. Most large businesses trademark their names to prevent other people from taking advantage of similar sounding names. For instance, try opening a restaurant named "McDonald's" even if McDonald is your real last name. You'll soon get a cease and desist letter from the attorneys for McDonald's Corporation - you know, that large fast-food chain. Don't try to mimic the name of a well known brand name or you're in for trouble. That includes not using slight misspellings of famous brands.

There is a final issue regarding your privacy when registering a domain name. As stated above you will be asked for the registrant's name, administrative contact, and technical contact. These can be the same. But you may be reluctant to put up your name and home address as the operator of a porn site since anyone in the world can view this information using a whois program. The good news is there are easy ways to get around this problem. Instead of listing your real first and last name, just substitute a generic names such as "The" and "Webmaster". If you have a business office address, you can list that but, again, there is no real legal requirement that this address be accurate. I never list my real home address. Instead I list an old home address. Even better I list a house number that doesn't exist which forces any junk mail to be returned to the sender. Believe me, no one sends you legitimate mail at the address listed in your whois information. For example, I used to live at 150 Cherry St., Bound Brook, NJ. So I list the whois address as 1500 Cherry St, etc. (I know there is no 1500 block on that street.) Some people don't even bother with this. They just enter obviously phony addresses or phone numbers with all zeros.

Your whois information is not the same as the credit card billing information that you will need to give in order to purchase a domain so don't feel that you have to use the same address. Purists will be aghast with this advice that you deliberate enter misleading whois data. Check it out for yourself, look at some whois listings at random particularly for adult sites, and you'll find many contain disguised information.   The one item that you need to give correctly is a working email contact address. This will enable someone to contact you if there is a genuine problem. Don't use your personal email address that you use on a daily basis. Create a special generic-sounding email address such as webmaster@youradultsitename.com for adult related correspondence. This helps to keep your real name anonymous. Your web hosting account will usually provide for creation of multiple email addresses If not, you can use the free mail services at Yahoo, Google, or Hotmail.

On the subject of email addresses, it is generally much better to use an address that is associated with your URL rather than a free email account. Free accounts suggest someone who is very cheap and on the fringe of the business just trying to get by. A genuine email address that reflects your website name suggests that you are legitimate businessman. In fact, many TGP and link list webmasters will not accept submissions from free web mail addresses for these very reasons. In the chapter on hosting, I'll tell you more about setting up your accounts.

After you've found a domain name, you can signup through any of the domain registrars. If you already have a hosting company account, you can usually signup through that company. In any event, there will a requirement that you locate your domain on a computer somewhere. All registrars offer some type of "parking" which is often free. This means that they temporarily locate your domain on one of their web servers with an "under construction" page. You can later move your domain to the hosting company of your choice. If you already have a hosting account when you register the domain, the host company will automatically locate your domain on one of their servers so no parking is needed.

Two good sources of general information about how the domain naming system works are the official sites for InterNic and ICANN. InterNIC offers information regarding domain name registration services and registrars. They also have a whois service. ICANN is the Internet Corporation for Assigned Names and Numbers. It is responsible for the global coordination of the Internet's unique identifiers including domain names (such as .com, .net, .org, .museum and country codes like .UK), as well as the addresses used in a variety of Internet protocols.

InterNIC
http://www.internic.net/

ICANN
http://icann.org/

Some registrars that I have used with success are listed below:

DirectNic
http://www.directnic.com/

Register
http://www.register.com/

GoDaddy
http://www.godaddy.com/

  These are but a drop in the bucket from the hundreds of registrars world wide. I recommend that you find one that you like and stick with it. Also, price is not the only factor to consider. Some offer incredibly cheap no-frills registrations for as little as $8.95 per year. Others such as DirectNic offer a host of extra features included in their $15.00 price. And some just charge a heck of a lot more for no known reason so shop around.

Hosting

There a hundreds of companies who provide website hosting. These can be categorized in several ways:

Paid Hosting

This is the most common arrangement. For a monthly fee your site is placed on one of the company's web servers with an Internet enabled connection. So you type in the name of your URL such as http://www.hotsexygirls.com and the browser will resolve that name to locate the files for your site on the web host's server. Whatever is in the files you created will be displayed. Hosting companies offer several options for accounts: type of server, bandwidth, amount of disk storage provided, and number of domains that can use the account.

There are three types of server accounts: shared virtual hosting, co-location hosting, or dedicated server hosting. Shared hosting means there are a number of different websites located on the same server. There may be hundreds of accounts on the same server. Each account is located in a "virtual" area which is somewhat like your email account. Your email account, wherever it may be located, is a virtual account that is shared with many other accounts. You can only see your email even though there are thousands or other user's messages on the same server. In the same way, with a shared hosting account you can see only your domain area.

Co-location means that you buy your own computer and configure it as a server. Then you ship if to the hosting company which basically rents you space and the Internet connection. A dedicated server means that you purchase an entire computer which is set up by the hosting company. Often this is just a single unit in a whole rack of servers at the host location. Both these methods are extremely expensive and complex. They are far beyond the needs of a beginning adult webmaster. Shared hosting is what you will need for your business.

The next factor is the amount of bandwidth provided. This refers to the amount of bytes of data that you can transfer through the Internet pipes. Adult sites use a lot of bandwidth because of high traffic (number of users) and the large file sizes needed for photos and video. Bandwidth is provided as a monthly allocation. For example, a small inexpensive shared account might allow up to one gigabyte of bandwidth per month. Go over the minimum and you'll pay a set fee for each additional gigabyte of traffic. If you find yourself regularly exceeding the minimum, your may want to switch to a different account that allows higher traffic. (This is just a switch on paper with your hosting company - you don't have to move your site.) In my experience bandwidth is not the problem that it used to be. As long as you stick with a host that specializes in adult hosting, its virtual accounts will provide adequate bandwidth.

Another factor for a hosting account is how much disk space you will have on the server. Adult sites require more space than others because of the large file sizes for pics and videos. The amount of space needed is exactly the same as the space used by your files on your own computer at home. Imagine that you create a site that uses one-half megabyte of file space on your desktop. That's exactly how much you'll need on the server. Fortunately, this isn't really much of a problem except with really cheap hosting accounts because adult hosting companies will provide adequate space for any beginning account.

Finally, a hosting account may be for a single domain name or it may allow a small number of domains on the same account. Avoid hosts that allow only a single domain. In that case you have to sign up for an additional account at additional monthly fee for each new website you bring online. Many hosts allow a moderate number of domains (5-10) on the same account. That way you pay nothing extra to add another site. After you reach the maximum you can add more sites by paying a small add-on fee each month. For example, my hosting company charges just 50 cents extra for each additional site after the first ten. It's important to select a host that allows multiple domains because our business model will call for creation of many sites. A paid hosting account need not be expensive. My provider has a starter account for $10 per month that allows up to five domains and five gigabytes of traffic which is enough to serve any beginning adult webmaster. There's tremendous competition among providers so shop around.

Free Hosting

Why pay for hosting at all when you can get it for free? As you'll see paid hosting is definitely better. There are two types of free hosting: small homepage websites that are provided free with some type of internet service account and advertising oriented free sites.

The first type is often provided by your Internet connection service. So for example, your cable modem provider might allow you to create a small site consisting of your homepage plus a limited number of additional pages. This is intended for low traffic sites of a personal nature. There are almost always restrictions on adult content because of objectionable material and the high traffic demands of porn sites. Usually these sites have a URL such as www.hostingcompanyname.com/~johndoe where your site is just a subdirectory of a larger site. Don't waste your time on this type of free site.

The second type is a site that derives its revenue from ads placed on your web pages. Typically, they insert a banner ad at the top and bottom of each page. The nature of these ads may be determined by the information you provide when you sign up with the host. Sites hosted on *Geocities* (geocities.com) and *Tripod* (tripod.com) are examples of advertising supported sites. They offer many of the features of paid hosting but on a smaller scale. Your domain registrar may also provide free advertising oriented hosting. Many of these free hosts will not accept adult websites so be sure to inquire before getting started. Otherwise, they may find out about you adult content when another user complains, and you'll get cancelled quickly. There are some ad-supported free hosts that accept and even specialize in adult content.

So what's the problem with free ad-oriented hosting? First, the sites often run very slow because they jam too many sites on a single server. Second, you have no control over the host's banners. Third, it doesn't look very businesslike and rather amateurish. Fourth, the host's banners may steal away business from you. If the user clicks on the host's banner, off he goes to some other place on the web, and he sure won't be around to sign up for a site you're promoting. A final problem and really a major one is that many link list and TGP operators will not accept submissions from free sites. They've had too many problems with free sites in the past and most have rules prohibiting them on their submission pages. So that eliminates some of your best sources of traffic.

The conclusion is that you need a paid virtual hosting account with a provider that accepts adult sites. Be sure to check the terms and conditions page before selecting a host because many exclude adult websites. On the other hand there are many hosts who'll be just happy to handle your adult traffic. Those that do have fast servers and powerful connections to the Internet backbone. This is the best way to make money: register your own domain name and pay for hosting services. Start with a small virtual host account. You can always add more disk space or bandwidth later.

In searching for a host, always look for the company's physical address somewhere on its website. Usually you'll find this on the homepage, a contacts page, or an "about us" page. Don't open an account with any provider that doesn't have a physical address. Also, you'll probably want a web host located in the same country where you are working. Hosting agreements are legal contracts - it helps for both parties to be in the same country. On the other hand, your host doesn't need to be physically located near you. I am located in the mid-western United States. My first host was in San Francisco, second in Florida, third in New York, and fourth in Philadelphia. You see is doesn't matter where they're located within your country as long as they have fast Internet connections. You would never actually need to go to the host's location. You will only make contact with your host via its website, via email, or by FTP file transfer.

Some hosting companies that I have used and recommend are listed below. There are many others. Just be sure the one you select does accept adult content.

Blue Gravity

http://www.bluegravity.com

WebAir

http://www.webair.com

Here are several sites that offer directories and reviews of adult hosting companies:

Adult TopHosts

http://adult.tophosts.com/

HostIndex

http://www.hostindex.com/

HostSearch

http://hostsearch.com/

Hosts4Porn

http://www.hosts4porn.com/

A Model Website

At last we'll go through the steps to build your first adult website. Based on this model you may create dozens or even hundreds of similar sites. Our site will use the name "Hot and Sexy Girls" with the URL assumed to be "hotsexygirls.com". As of the time of this writing, that URL is actually not in use but someone may purchase it at any time. Therefore, if you type in this URL into a web browser, you may get an entirely different site. In the examples below, you'll see the page as it looks, and I've simply blocked out space for the advertising banners since these will vary with the sponsors you choose. After each page is a discussion of the HTML code (hypertext markup language) used to produce the page.

There are at least four pages in this site depending upon how many galleries you use:

Warning Page

This serves as an introduction to the site. It contains a paragraph warning to users that this is an adult site containing nudity and other content of a sexual nature. It warns persons under the age of 18 that they may not proceed further into the site. I would try to avoid any nudity on this page or at least limit it to the topless type. (Also avoid nudity in the banners placed on this page.) The page will have a couple of advertising banners because you want the user to go to a pay site as soon as possible. If he clicks to go to a pay site immediately on the first page, so what if he never comes back to view your site. This is a little like putting some ads in the paper or on a billboard. Their purpose is to get the customer to go to the store. Another essential element on the warning page is an Entry Link that leads to the Main Page of your site. This is usually right under the warning paragraph. It implies that the user is agreeing to the terms of the warning by clicking the Entry Link. It can also have an Exit Link that routes the user to some other place if he doesn't agree to the terms. This link might to go a search engine such as *Google*. Better still, it can lead to some non-adult money making sponsor. Amazon.com offers affiliate programs for books and merchandise sales. Let your exit traffic go to *Amazon* and maybe you'll get an unexpected sale. Or send your surfers to a DVD site. Try to choose an exit site the will appeal to the average porn surfer.

Near the bottom should be some text regarding your compliance with any 2257 regulations and a copyright notice. Sure, you want to claim a copyright on your site. This is mainly to scare off other webmasters from directly copying your pages. I once had a site named "TeenieMax." Much to my amazement, after several years I found there was a Japanese site with the same name that was using some of my source code and keywords. I found this by searching on "TeenieMax" in a search engine. The discovery didn't really matter to me at the time because I wasn't seeking Japanese traffic and so the copied site wasn't really a competitor.

Main Page

This is the heart of your site - a menu to the other pages. It will contain several advertising banners and text links promoting sponsor sites. At the top will be a logo for your site if you care to create one or just the name of the site perhaps in a box with contrasting text and background. Somewhere near the middle of the page and underneath at least two advertising banners will be the links that go your galleries. Some webmasters use text links such as "Gallery 1", "Gallery 2", etc. I prefer to use a thumbnail image of the girl who is featured in each gallery. Just a head and shoulders or head and tits shot is all you need for the thumbnail. I usually give each girl a name, silly as that is, and include it in a text link directly under the thumbnail.

Two Gallery Pages

There will be a single page for each model you are featuring. Each gallery will again have your logo or site name at the top. There will be 2-4 advertising banners. Somewhere in the middle will be the 12-16 thumbnail images that are linked to the full-sized pictures. There is a minimum of two Gallery Pages in order to get accepted by link sites although I often use up to four galleries.

Some Specifics about the Warning Page

1. This file is usually named "index.htm", "index.html", or "default.htm" depending upon the type of web server you are using. This is a default file name that the server will display if no file is specified. Check with your hosting company if in doubt. For example, if you type in http://www.hotsexygirls.com/ without a filename, the default page will automatically be displayed.

2. The warning page has a small image, preferably of a clothed model, or a logo at the top. This helps to establish the mood of the site and give the surfer a preview teaser about the content inside. Include the name of the site in largest text near the top. This is important for search engine robots to find your site name first. The name should also appear as the first thing in the browser title.

3. Directly under the title display and image, place some keyword-rich text that describes the site with words that will help the search engine robots to understand what your site is about. A paragraph or so is fine.

4. You can use several sponsors' banners on the index page placing them as I have shown. Banners could actually be larger than the examples.

5. You need a copyright and 2257 statement. Again, I am not a lawyer. Mine looks like this:

"All photos are copyrighted by the Site Owner or the photographers who supply original material to this site. All photos are legally licensed to this site. Any commercial use of this copyrighted material without prior licensing is forbidden by Federal Law. All models are 18 years of age or older. All records required by 18 USC 2257 are in the custody of the Site Owner or its photographers."

6. You need a warning text. Just as movies display a rating at the start and television networks display warnings about mature or graphic images, the web site warning throws the responsibility on the viewer whether to enter or not. While the legal strength of warning pages has never been tested conclusively in the courts, it is a first step in showing that you are a responsible webmaster. Notice how I have placed some of the warning in a scrolling textbox which goes just above the entry link. (The text is shown below.) I am not a lawyer so don't assume my example is the best.

7. There's no law requiring a Warning Page but for legal reasons it's certainly a good idea. Some search engines and directories will not list your site without a warning. It is also required by many free adult web hosts and adult verification networks. Look at the Warning Page as a good thing because you can include several large advertising banners and text links without having to display any expensive porn content.

A Sample Warning Message

This website is an adult entertainment and educational resource not designed to promote prurient interests. This warning page constitutes a legal Agreement between yourself and the site owner.

1. I am at least 18 years of age.

2. The sexually explicit material I am buying and/or viewing is for my own personal use and I will never expose minors to said material.

3. I am not a U.S. Postal official, or law enforcement agent, or acting as an agent thereof, attempting to obtain any evidence for the prosecution of any individual or corporation, or for the purpose of entrapment.

4. I desire to receive and haven't notified the U.S. Postal Service, or any other governmental agency to intercept sexually explicit material.

5. I believe that, as an adult, I have the unalienable right to read and/or view any type of material that I choose and that the material and images contained in this website are not obscene or offensive in any way, nor could ever be construed to be obscene or offensive.

6. The viewing, reading, and downloading of the material and images in this website do not violate the community standards of my street, village, city, town, county, state, province, or country.

7. That I am wholly liable for any false disclosures and responsible for any legal ramifications that may arise from viewing, reading, or downloading of material and images contained within this website and that webmaster, and its affiliates cannot be held responsible for any legal ramifications that may arise as a result of fraudulent entry into, or use of, this website and/or material contain herein.

Sample Warning Page

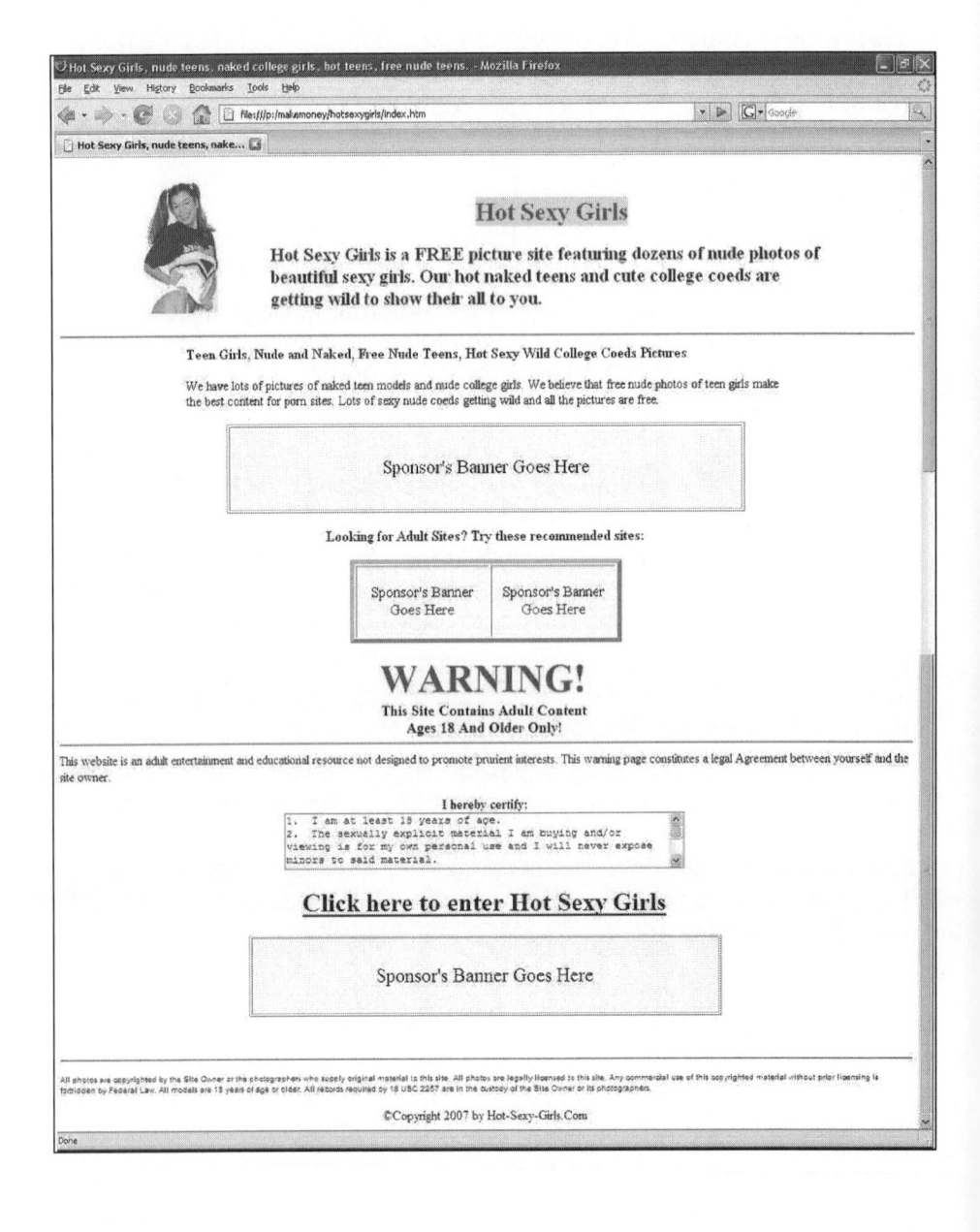

Some Specifics About The Main Page

1. Be sure to include your site title in the browser's title tag. You can include your logo or image along with a short descriptive text again at the top of this page. The filename for this page can be anything you want such as "main.htm". Sometimes I use the name of the site with words separated by underscores as the filename. For example, your Main Page might be named "hot_sexy_girls.htm". Some experts in search engine optimization feel that use of keywords in filenames may get a higher position in their search engine listings.

2. Three or four banners will go well on this page. This is where the surfer will spend most of his time so give him every opportunity to visit a sponsor's pay site.

3. Include a copyright notice at the bottom for your protection.

4. Keep in mind that the purpose of this page and subsequent gallery pages is to entice the surfer to visit one of your sponsor's pay sites. In addition to attractive banners, there should be text suggesting there's more and better stuff at the pay site. I have stopped showing hardcore photos at all on free sites. Too much hard porn defeats your purpose - you want the viewer to click through to the pay site to get his hardcore stuff. Video clips that are served up by your sponsor are usually OK because they suck the surfer right up into the pay site.

5. Use your image compression program to optimize the graphics on your pages. Many webmasters don't realize that images are often bloated to excess file sizes. These can be compressed just to the point before they begin to degrade. This will result in much faster loading times for your pages. Sponsor-provided banners are notorious for bloat. You'll find sponsor banners that are 40,000 bytes in size. A good compression program can reduce those banners to maybe 25,000 bytes and save you a little load time. Do the same compression with your own logos. Also, resizing logos and banners to make them a little smaller will speed up your loading process.

Sample Main Page

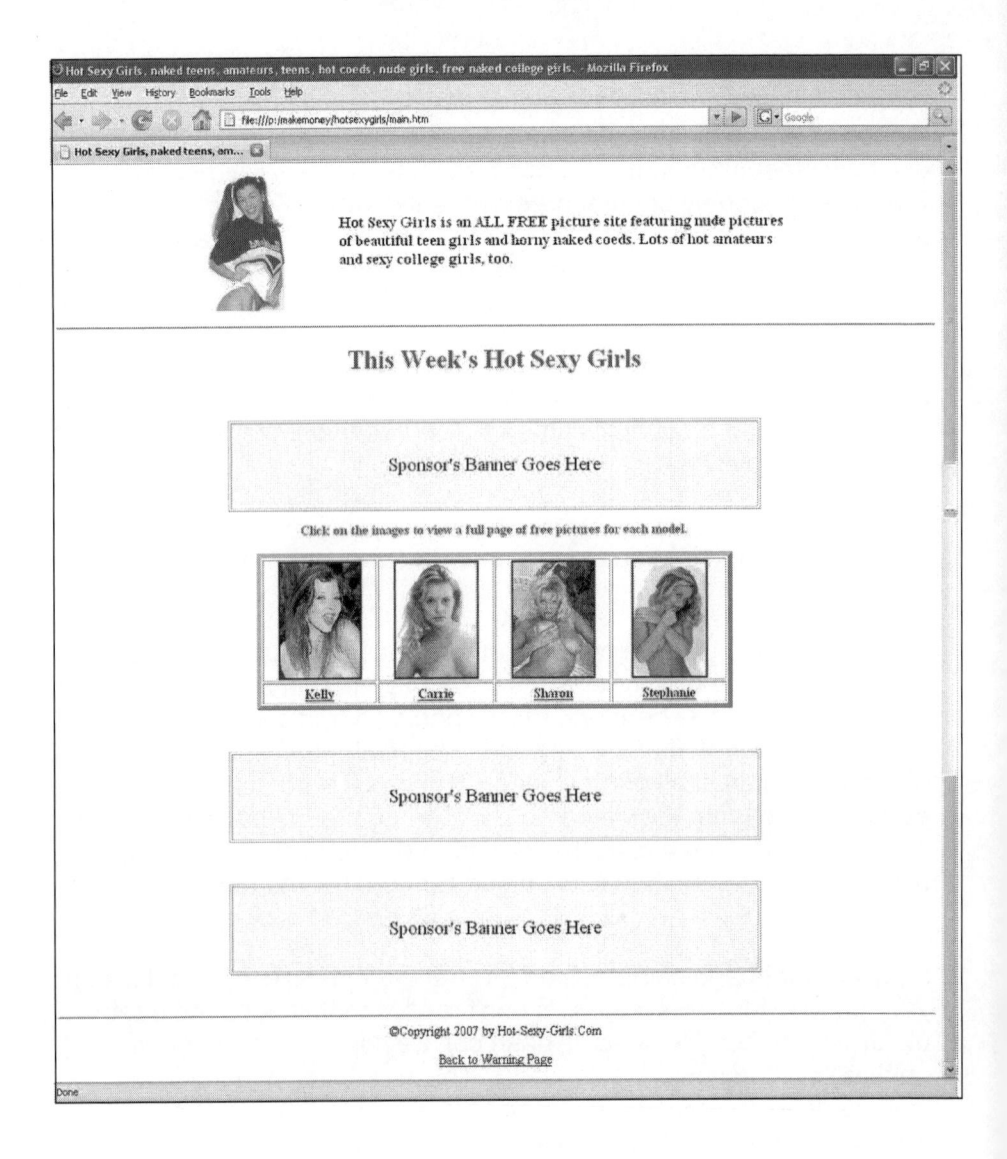

Sample Gallery Page

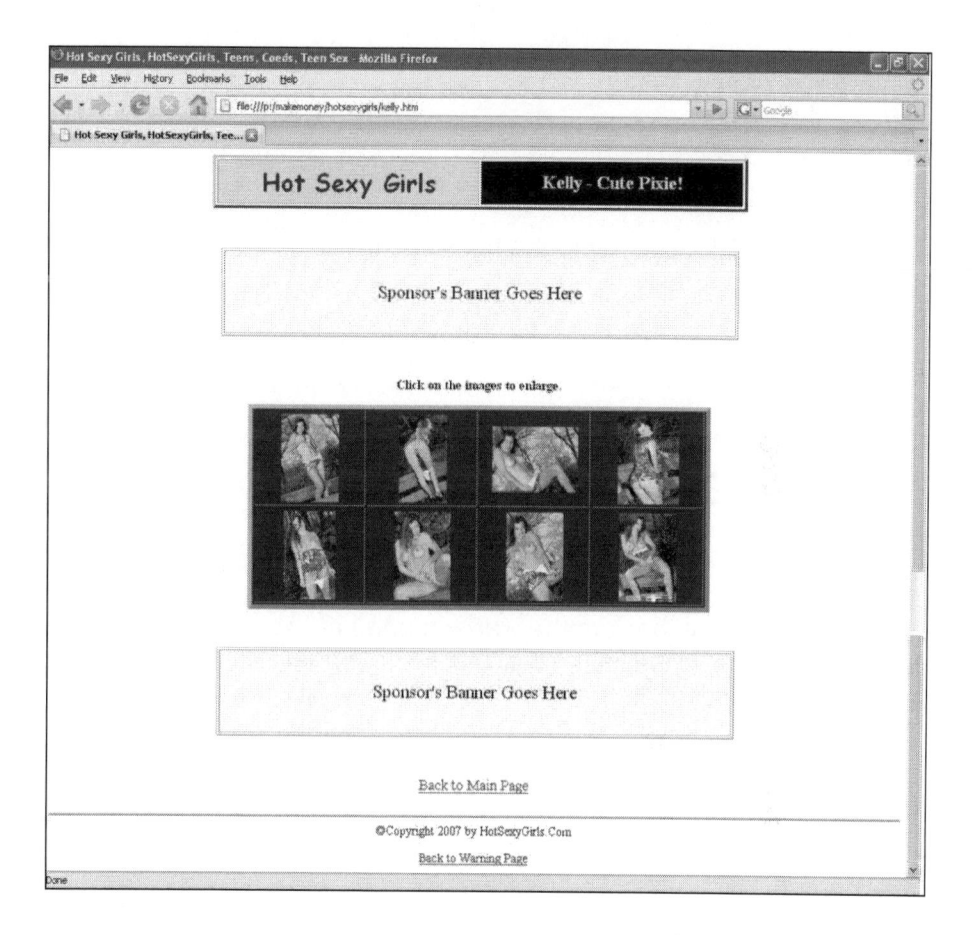

Some Specifics About The Gallery Pages

1. You will have 2-4 galleries. In this example there are only eight thumbnails rather than sixteen because the main page links to four galleries for a total of 32 pics. If you have sixteen pics in each gallery, they can be used almost "as is" for TGP submissions.

2. Each thumb links directly to the full-sized photo.

3. Include your site title at the top and in the browser title tag.

4. Don't use more than two banners on the gallery pages or some link lists may reject your site.

5. Notice that there is a link back to the previous page at the bottom of the gallery. This helps to make your site more user friendly. I usually stick in a link back to the warning page at the very bottom. Some people feel these links help to achieve higher rankings with search engine optimization.

Warning Page Source Code

```html
<HTML><HEAD>
<TITLE>Hot Sexy Girls, nude teens, naked college girls, hot teens, free nude teens.</TITLE>

<META NAME="Classification" CONTENT="Adult">

<META NAME="Description" CONTENT="Hot Sexy Girls is the ultimate place for free pictures of nude teen girls. Hot sexy teens and college girls all nude and naked showing off for you.">

<META NAME="keywords" CONTENT="sexy girls, nude teens, college girls, hot teens, nude, free nude teens, teen girl, teen sex, nude coeds, free pics, nude teens, nude pics, coeds, naked teens">

</HEAD>

<BODY>
<CENTER>
<TABLE><TR>
<TD WIDTH=150>
<IMG SRC="images\monica1.jpg" ALIGN=LEFT BORDER=0 ALT="Hot Sexy Girls, Nude Teens, Naked Girls">
</TD>
<TD WIDTH=650>
<P><BR>
<CENTER><H1><FONT COLOR=RED>
<B style="background:YELLOW">Hot Sexy Girls</B style="background:WHITE"></FONT></H1></CENTER>
<P>
<H2><FONT COLOR=BLUE><B>
Hot Sexy Girls is a FREE picture site featuring dozens of nude photos of beautiful sexy girls. Our hot naked teens and cute college coeds are getting wild to show their all to you.
</B></FONT></H2>
</TD>
</TR></TABLE>

<HR NOSHADE>

<TABLE WIDTH=700><TR><TD>
```

```html
<H3>Teen Girls, Nude and Naked, Free Nude Teens, Hot Sexy Wild College Coeds Pictures</H3></FONT>

We have lots of pictures of naked teen models and nude college girls. We believe that free nude photos of teen girls make the best content for porn sites. Lots of sexy nude coeds getting wild and all the pictures are free.


</TD></TR></TABLE></CENTER>


<P><CENTER>
<TABLE WIDTH=600 HEIGHT=100 BORDER=1><TR><TD ALIGN=CENTER BGCOLOR=LIGHTYELLOW>
<FONT SIZE=5>Sponsor's Banner Goes Here</FONT>
</TD></TR></TABLE>
</CENTER>


<P>
<CENTER><H3>Looking for Adult Sites?  Try these recommended sites:</H3>
<TABLE BORDER=5 BGCOLOR="LIGHTYELLOW">
  <TR ALIGN=CENTER>
    <TD WIDTH=150 HEIGHT=80 ALIGN=CENTER>
      <FONT SIZE=4>Sponsor's Banner Goes Here</FONT>
    </TD>
    <TD WIDTH=140 HEIGHT=80 ALIGN=CENTER>
      <FONT SIZE=4>Sponsor's Banner Goes Here</FONT>
    </TD>
  </TR>
</TABLE></CENTER>


<P><CENTER>
<FONT COLOR="RED" SIZE="8"><B>WARNING!</B></FONT>
<BR>
<FONT COLOR="BLACK" SIZE="4"><B>
This Site Contains Adult Content<BR>
Ages 18 And Older Only!</B></FONT>
</CENTER>


<HR NOSHADE>

This website is an adult entertainment and educational resource not designed to promote prurient interests.  This warning page constitutes a legal Agreement between yourself and the site owner.
```

```html
<P><CENTER>
<B>I hereby certify:</B>
<FORM>
<TEXTAREA NAME="certify" ROWS=3 COLS=60>
```
1. I am at least 18 years of age.

2. The sexually explicit material I am buying and/or viewing is for my own personal use and I will never expose minors to said material.

3. I am not a U.S. Postal official, or law enforcement agent, or acting as an agent thereof, attempting to obtain any evidence for the prosecution of any individual or corporation, or for the purpose of entrapment.

4. I desire to receive and haven't notified the U.S. Postal Service, or any other governmental agency to intercept sexually explicit material.

5. I believe that, as an adult, I have the unalienable right to read and/or view any type of material that I choose and that the material and images contained in this website are not obscene or offensive in any way, nor could ever be construed to be obscene or offensive.

6. The viewing, reading, and downloading of the material and images in this website do not violate the community standards of my street, village, city, town, county, state, province, or country.

7. That I am wholly liable for any false disclosures and responsible for any legal ramifications that may arise from viewing, reading, or downloading of material and images contained within this website and that VentureHosts, and its affiliates cannot be held responsible for any legal ramifications that may arise as a result of fraudulent entry into, or use of, this website and/or material contain herein.

```html
</TEXTAREA></CENTER>
</FORM>

<P><CENTER>
<H1><A HREF="main.htm"><B>Click here to enter Hot Sexy Girls</B></A></H1>
</CENTER>

<P><CENTER>
<TABLE WIDTH=600 HEIGHT=100 BORDER=1><TR><TD ALIGN=CENTER BGCOLOR=LIGHTYELLOW>
<FONT SIZE=5>Sponsor's Banner Goes Here</FONT>
</TD></TR></TABLE>
</CENTER>

<P><BR>
<HR NOSHADE>

<P><FONT SIZE="1" FACE="arial">All photos are copyrighted by the Site Owner or the photographers who supply original material to this site. All photos are legally licensed to this
```

site. Any commercial use of this copyrighted material without prior licensing is forbidden by Federal Law. All models are 18 years of age or older. All records required by 18 USC 2257 are in the custody of the Site Owner or its photographers.</FONT>

<P><CENTER>©Copyright 2007 by Hot-Sexy-Girls.Com</CENTER>

</BODY>
</HTML>

Main Page Source Code

```
<HTML><HEAD>

<TITLE>Hot Sexy Girls, naked teens, amateurs, teens, hot coeds, nude girls, free naked college girls.</TITLE>

<META NAME="Description" CONTENT="Hot Sexy Girls is the ultimate place for free pictures of beautiful nude teen girls and horny naked coeds! These sexy college girls will do anything to please.">

<META NAME="keywords" CONTENT="hot sexy girls, sexy girls, nude, teens, teen, teen girl, teen sex, nude teen">

</HEAD>

<BODY BGCOLOR=WHITE>

<CENTER>
<TABLE BORDER=0 BGCOLOR=WHITE>
 <TR>
   <TD WIDTH=150>
     <IMG SRC="images/monica1.jpg" ALIGN=LEFT ALT="Hot-Sexy-Girls.Com">
   </TD>
   <TD WIDTH=500>
     <FONT COLOR=BLACK SIZE=4><B>
     Hot Sexy Girls is an ALL FREE picture site featuring nude pictures
     of beautiful teen girls and horny naked coeds. Lots of hot amateurs
     and sexy college girls, too.</B>
     </FONT>
   </TD>
 </TR>
</TABLE></CENTER>

<P>
<HR NOSHADE>

<CENTER>
<FONT COLOR="RED">
```

```html
<H1>This Week's Hot Sexy Girls</H1>
</FONT></CENTER>


<P><BR><CENTER>
<TABLE WIDTH=600 HEIGHT=100 BORDER=1><TR><TD ALIGN=CENTER BGCOLOR=LIGHTYELLOW>
<FONT SIZE=5 COLOR=BLACK>Sponsor's Banner Goes Here</FONT>
</TD></TR></TABLE>
</CENTER>


<P><BR><CENTER>
<TABLE WIDTH=600 HEIGHT=100 BORDER=1><TR><TD ALIGN=CENTER BGCOLOR=LIGHTYELLOW>
<FONT SIZE=5 COLOR=BLACK>Sponsor's Banner Goes Here</FONT>
</TD></TR></TABLE>
</CENTER>


<P><BR><CENTER>
<FONT COLOR=RED>
<B>Click on the images to view a full page of free pictures for each model.</B></FONT></CENTER>
<BR>
<CENTER>
<TABLE BORDER=5>
 <TR ALIGN=CENTER>
   <TD WIDTH=125><A HREF="kelly.htm"><IMG SRC="images/kelly08.125" WIDTH=90 HEIGHT=125 ALT="Sexy Girls, Free Pics, Teens, Coeds"></A></TD>
   <TD WIDTH=125><A HREF="carrie.htm"><IMG SRC="images/carrie07.125" WIDTH=90 HEIGHT=125 ALT="Sexy Girls, Free Pics, Teens, Coeds"></A></TD>
   <TD WIDTH=125><A HREF="sharon.htm"><IMG SRC="images/sharon12.125" WIDTH=90 HEIGHT=125 ALT="Sexy Girls, Free Pics, Teens, Coeds"></A></TD>
   <TD WIDTH=125><A HREF="steph.htm"><IMG SRC="images/steph03.125" WIDTH=82 HEIGHT=125 ALT="Sexy Girls, Free Pics, Teens, Coeds"></A></TD>
 </TR>

 <TR ALIGN=CENTER>
  <TD><A HREF="kelly.htm"><B>Kelly</B></A></TD>
  <TD><A HREF="carrie.htm"><B>Carrie</B></A></TD>
  <TD><A HREF="sharon.htm"><B>Sharon</B></A></TD>
  <TD><A HREF="steph.htm"><B>Stephanie</B></A></TD>
 </TR>
</TABLE>
```

```
</CENTER>

<P><BR><CENTER>
<TABLE WIDTH=600 HEIGHT=100 BORDER=1><TR><TD ALIGN=CENTER BGCOLOR=LIGHTYELLOW>
<FONT SIZE=5 COLOR=BLACK>Sponsor's Banner Goes Here</FONT>
</TD></TR></TABLE>
</CENTER>


<P><BR><CENTER>
<TABLE WIDTH=600 HEIGHT=100 BORDER=1><TR><TD ALIGN=CENTER BGCOLOR=LIGHTYELLOW>
<FONT SIZE=5 COLOR=BLACK>Sponsor's Banner Goes Here</FONT>
</TD></TR></TABLE>
</CENTER>

<P><BR>
<HR NOSHADE>


<CENTER>&copy;Copyright 2007 by Hot-Sexy-Girls.Com

<P><A HREF="index.htm">Back to Warning Page</A></CENTER>

</BODY>
</HTML>
```

Gallery Page Source Code

```
<HTML><HEAD>
<TITLE>Hot Sexy Girls, HotSexyGirls, Teens, Coeds, Teen Sex</TITLE>
</HEAD>

<BODY BGCOLOR=WHITE TEXT=BLACK LINK=BLUE ALINK=RED VLINK=RED>

<CENTER><TABLE BORDER=3 BORDERCOLOR=RED>
<TR ALIGN=CENTER>
   <TD WIDTH=300 HEIGHT=50 BGCOLOR=YELLOW>
     <FONT COLOR=BLUE SIZE=6 FACE='COMIC SANS MS'>
     <B>Hot Sexy Girls</B></FONT>
     </FONT>
   </TD>
   <TD WIDTH=300 BGCOLOR=BLACK>
     <FONT COLOR=YELLOW SIZE=5><B>
     Kelly - Cute Pixie!
     </B></FONT>
   </TD>
</TR>
</TABLE></CENTER><P>


<P><BR><CENTER>
<TABLE WIDTH=600 HEIGHT=100 BORDER=1><TR><TD ALIGN=CENTER BGCOLOR=LIGHTYELLOW>
<FONT SIZE=5>Sponsor's Banner Goes Here</FONT>
</TD></TR></TABLE>
</CENTER>


<P><BR><CENTER>
<B>Click on the images to enlarge.</B>


<P>
<TABLE BORDER=5 BGCOLOR="BLUE">
  <TR ALIGN=CENTER>
    <TD WIDTH=125><A HREF="images/kelly01.jpg"><IMG SRC="images/kelly01.100" ALT="Sexy Girls, Free Pics, Teens, Coeds"></A></TD>
```

```html
   <TD WIDTH=125><A HREF="images/kelly03.jpg"><IMG SRC="images/kelly03.100" ALT="Sexy Girls, Free Pics, Teens, Coeds" ></A></TD>
   <TD WIDTH=125><A HREF="images/kelly04.jpg"><IMG SRC="images/kelly04.100" ALT="Sexy Girls, Free Pics, Teens, Coeds"></A></TD>
   <TD WIDTH=125><A HREF="images/kelly05.jpg"><IMG SRC="images/kelly05.100" ALT="Sexy Girls, Free Pics, Teens, Coeds"></A></TD>
 </TR>
 <TR ALIGN=CENTER>
   <TD WIDTH=125><A HREF="images/kelly12.jpg"><IMG SRC="images/kelly12.100" ALT="Sexy Girls, Free Pics, Teens, Coeds"></A></TD>
   <TD WIDTH=125><A HREF="images/kelly07.jpg"><IMG SRC="images/kelly07.100" ALT="Sexy Girls, Free Pics, Teens, Coeds"></A></TD>
   <TD WIDTH=125><A HREF="images/kelly09.jpg"><IMG SRC="images/kelly09.100" ALT="Sexy Girls, Free Pics, Teens, Coeds"></A></TD>
   <TD WIDTH=125><A HREF="images/kelly10.jpg"><IMG SRC="images/kelly10.100" ALT="Sexy Girls, Free Pics, Teens, Coeds"></A></TD>
 </TR>
</TABLE>
</CENTER>

<P><BR><CENTER>
<TABLE WIDTH=600 HEIGHT=100 BORDER=1><TR><TD ALIGN=CENTER BGCOLOR=LIGHTYELLOW>
<FONT SIZE=5>Sponsor's Banner Goes Here</FONT>
</TD></TR></TABLE>
</CENTER>

<P><BR><CENTER>
<A HREF="main.htm"><FONT SIZE=4>Back to Main Page</FONT></A></CENTER>
<BR><HR NOSHADE>
<CENTER>&COPY;Copyright 2007 by HotSexyGirls.Com</CENTER>

<P><CENTER><A HREF="index.htm">Back to Warning Page</A></CENTER>

</BODY>
</HTML>
```

Some Thoughts About HTML Coding

This document cannot begin to teach you the art of writing HTML code. There are any number of good books for this purpose. The code for our three sample pages is shown below. The Warning Page (index.htm) is by far the most important because search engines consider it first in determining your site ranking. All HTML code needs to be written carefully and checked for correctness with search engines in mind. Here are some elements of coding to observe:

1. Note the text of the <TITLE> tag on each page. This is most important for search engine rankings. Note how this tag is closed with </TITLE>. Most other tags also have and opening and closing tag.

2. Note the text of the <META NAME="Description" tag. This description will often be picked up by the SE robot and used for the textual description of your site in the search engine results page. Note how the description prominently uses some of the same words that are found in the title.

3. Note the text of the <META NAME="keywords" tag. These terms will be filed away by the SE robot to categorize your site in its database. The terms are comma delimited in this listing so "sexy girls" will be treated as one keyword. You can include single words such as "sexy" but their likelihood of ever being found is limited because there are just too many single words. Keywords should really be short two and three word phrases that are distinctive.

4. In the body of the code which begins with the <BODY> tag, note how the text is categorized into different size fonts by use of the header tags: <H1> = largest, <H2> = large, and <H3> = normal. The <H1> text contains our site title which appears in the largest font on

the page. The <H2> text contains important descriptive information. The <H3> text is still more descriptive information but less important than <H1> or <H2>. Figure that a search engine robot will consider the text in the top half of your page to be the most important and use the header tags to further differentiate as the robot tries to determine what you page is about.

4. Robots do not read images, by the way, so putting "Hot Sexy Girls" in huge text in an image will help you in no way. However, you can include an <ALT= tag with each image as shown here, and the robot will read it:

<IMG SRC="yourimagename.jpg" ALT="Hot Sexy Girls, Nude Teens, Naked Girls">

5. Note use of the paragraph <P> and new line <BR> tags to separate various objects on the page. These are usually used together like so: <P>
 which gives the effect of a double space. Use these to create white space on your page so things aren't crowded too close together. Also note the use of the <CENTER> tag and its closer </CENTER> to insure that content is centered. You need these because the surfer's computer screen may not be set to the same resolution as yours. The <CENTER> tags will make sure things stay lined up as you envisioned them.

6. I use <HR NOSHADE> sometimes to draw a horizontal line across the page. This is optional. It sometimes helps to separate different elements of page content.

7. The most important HTML coding feature that you need to learn is the <TABLE> tag. As you study one of the HTML books, spend extra time with the chapter on tables. They are used for all kinds of purposes to set off content and especially images such as thumbnails. You'll see several tables on the Warning Page. They're also around the thumbnails on the Main Page and the Gallery Page.

8. The font size of the text on your page can be controlled by the <FONT> tag and its closer </FONT>. This is mainly used to determine the size of the text from 1 = very small to 6 = very large.

You can also designate a color (from a standard list of colors) if you want something other that the default text color. For example: <FONT SIZE=5 COLOR=RED> will give you red text in a fairly large size.

9. Note the use of the <BODY> tag in the following statement:

<BODY BGCOLOR=WHITE TEXT=BLACK LINK=BLUE ALINK=RED VLINK=RED>

The optional property elements give you more control over the page:

BGCOLOR=WHITE	page background will be white
TEXT=BLACK	default text will be black
LINK=BLUE	hypertext links to other pages will be blue
ALINK=RED	while selected link will be red
VLINK=RED	visited links will be red

Suppose we change the <BODY> tag as follows:

<BODY BGCOLOR=BLACK TEXT=WHITE LINK=YELLOW ALINK=CYAN VLINK=CYAN>

Now we have a black screen with white text and yellow links. Links that have already been visited will be cyan. Black screens are very common in adult sites. Just be sure you set you text to something other than the default black color, or the text won't be visible. Experiment with various colors but always with a mind to improving readability. Some of the worst pages I've seen have blue text on a black background because the text is almost always hard to read. Use colors that pop out against the background to emphasize important text.

10. Get yourself a script checking program for HTML code. These come as part of many standard code editors such as *Dreamweaver*.

An excellent free program that can be used with any editor is *CSE HTML Validator Lite*. This can be downloaded at the following URL:

CSE HTML Validator Lite

http://www.htmlvalidator.com/lite/

Although this product offers more expensive deluxe versions, I have never found any need to go beyond the free version. Always check your code. It's very easy to make a mistake by a typo or leaving out a tag. Many browsers will accommodate some coding omissions and thus fool you into thinking everything is fine. But the browser your surfer is using may see every mistake as an error. Also, search engine robots may be foiled by HTML errors and bypass your page. So be sure to check your final version of the code before putting it up on your website. Because browsers render pages slightly differently, I usually check my pages with both Internet Explorer and FireFox.

Sources of Traffic

Traffic means the hits that you get to your Internet site pages. It is the lifeblood of your business. Imagine that you have written a novel. Traffic would be the customers who pick up your book in a bookstore or seek it out on *amazon.com*. Without traffic, there can be no sales. In this chapter we will look at various ways to bring hits to your website. We will assume that you have opened up a new free site called "hotsexygirls.com" (a made-up name by the way), and the site's now on your hosted server account. In other words, entering http://hotsexygirls.com in a browser will bring up your site. There are many sources of traffic and you can buy whole books about the subject of generating traffic. Some of the most important sources for adult webmasters are discussed below.

Search Engines

The major search engines such as Google, Yahoo, Ask, Alta Vista, AOL Search, and MSN Search provide some of the best traffic possible. This engines display lists of site URLs that match the keywords entered by a surfer. For example, go to Google and enter the keywords "hot sexy girls", and a number of pages will be returned listing sites where those words are prominent. How does a search engine find and evaluate these sites? It has a database of relevant information about literally millions of sites.

Search engines obtain data in two basic ways: robot programs and user submissions. A robot program is a highly specialized computer program that constantly traverses the World Wide Web moving from site to site by following the links in finds on web pages. As it reaches the first page each site, it is particularly interested in the text on that page in order to find out what the site is about and begins categorizing it in the database. Then it searches through a number of additional pages that are linked off the first page. All this information is stored in the database according to a complex algorithm that varies with each search engine. The algorithm is proprietary information that is the heart of the search engine. The second method of obtaining data is from users like you. In the early days of the web, all search engines had a suggestions page where users could submit a page to be considered for inclusion in the database. The person making the suggestion is usually associated with the submitted site, but this wasn't always true. After receiving a submission, either the robot or a live person would look at the site to determine if it was appropriate. Nowadays, many of the search engines no longer actively accept submissions from users. They prefer to locate new sites with their robots. It is assumed that a new site will be linked from other sites if it is truly important, and the robots will sooner or later traverse these links to find the site.

In the 2000's, most of the search engine companies came to realize that accepting site submissions directly from webmasters could be a profitable business in itself. Instead of offering a free site submission page, they switched to the paid submission business model. Here the webmaster submits his site for consideration along with a fee that may be as much as several hundred dollars. Incidentally, the fee is not returned if they don't accept your site. As you can see, paying for submission to a search engine can get expensive very fast. It's not something we want to include in our business model so we must stick to search engines that still have free submission pages.

The site you submit to any search engine will be among thousands of pages submitted in a single day. So how do you get your site to the top of the heap? This is done by a process called "search engine optimization" or SEO. There are whole books written about SEO and plenty of websites discussing the best ways to optimize a page. The optimization process may differ slightly for each search engine. A page that rates really high in Google may be slightly different from a highly ranked page in Yahoo. However, there are enough common ranking principles that can be used to create a page that meets the standards of most search engines.

The most important SEO elements are keywords in the page title and the preponderance of those keywords in the body of text on the page. In addition, the font size of the keywords and placement of the page will have an effect. In our imaginary site, we will want the phrase "hot sexy girls" in the title that appears at the top of the browser. We will also want the phrase in a large font type at the top of the page. Further down on the page will be several paragraphs that constitute the body of text for that page, and within those paragraphs we should find the words "hot", "sexy" and "girls" interspersed within the text. Robots actually count the number of occurrences of the various keywords on a page. It is assumed that the more important words will appear more times on the page so we would want our keywords to appear maybe half a dozen times. This enables a dumb computer robot program to reach certain conclusions about the subject of the page. In this case we want the robot to assume our page is about "hot, sexy, girls".

What about images on the page? OK, so you've used your image editor to prepare some pics of lovely looking girls that are interspersed about your page. Images don't count for much with search engines because the robots can't read them. However, with each image you can include an "alt" tag in the code. The text of this tag is displayed when the user's mouse hovers over the image. Alt tags are usually read by robots so here we might want to include a tag like this:

alt = "Free Hot Sexy Girls, Nude Teens, Naked, College Girls Naked"

Another type of tag is the "meta" tag that is placed in code near the top of the page. Meta tags are not displayed by the browser at all. They are invisible descriptive tags placed in the page's source code to help search engines uncover what the page is about. There are two types: meta description and meta keywords. Here are some actual examples:

<META NAME="Description" CONTENT="Hot-n-sexy-girls has pictures of beautiful naked college girls and hot nude teen girls.">

<META NAME="keywords" CONTENT="free hot girls, hot girls, nude teen girl, free teens, free nude teens, hot, free pics, teen girls, teen sex, college girls, naked teens, nude teens, nude pics, coeds">

The description tag may be picked up by the robot and stored literally as the description of you site that appears in the search engine results. The keywords are stored in the database to help the engine find appropriate pages to match the keywords that the user has submitted in his search request. These meta tags go in the Header section of the webpage.

As soon as you have your Warning Page fully optimized for search engines and the rest of the site at least in acceptable form, you should go ahead and submit to the search engines. (Only submit the Warning Page as the SE robot will follow your internal links to the other pages.) There are two reasons to get submitted early:

1. Many search engines take a long time to get around to scanning your site so the sooner you get on their list, the sooner you'll get into the SE results. Directories that use humans to view your site will take even longer.

2. Search engines consider your first page to be the most important. If your Warning Page is well optimized, that's where they'll get most of the data for your listing. The robots do scan deeper into a site but many only look at the top few pages on their first transversal of a new site.

One of the neat things about search engines is that your pages seem to last forever as long as they remain on your server. I've found pages submitted four or five years ago popping up in search results, and these can bring traffic long after you've forgotten them. Just make sure the links to your sponsors remain current on those old pages. Sometimes sponsors go out of business or modify their linking requirements. Keep those old pages updated so you don't inadvertently lose some business.

Do not use automated submission programs to submit to search engines. Although convenient, these programs can generate red flags for major search engines since they are often used to submit spam pages. These programs can get your site URL temporarily blacklisted by the search engine. Once you submit to a particular engine, you don't have to keep resubmitting the same page. Be patient - it may take several weeks for your page to appear in the listings.

Any time you make significant changes to your page, it may be good to resubmit it because search engines do like new content and will track pages that are frequently updated more often than static ones. If your page is indexed but not ranking very well, try linking the page to/from pages that are ranking better. Google recommends that rather than submit individual pages, to link them to the main pages of your site and let the crawler index them as they are found.

If you have a page that is regularly updated, and you'd like the search robots to visit it more often, there is a trick to try. Include a meta tag like this in your page header:

<Meta name="revisit after" content="7-days">

This tells the SE robot to revisit the page every seven days. Also, modifying your page slightly on a regular basis will cause the robots to visit more frequently. Each time you save your file, the file's date property is set to a new date, and robots recognize this change and will re-index the page.

Search engine algorithms are constantly changing. Keep current on the latest techniques for optimization by regularly visiting some of the search engine optimization sites and forums that a listing in the Getting Help chapter. Two forums that I particularly like and view weekly are as follows:

SearchEngineWatch Forums
http://forums.searchenginewatch.com/index.php

High Rankings Forums
http://www.highrankings.com/forum/

Search engine optimization is a most important skill that you need to learn in order to become a successful adult webmaster. Search engines are usually thought to provide one of the best types of traffic since the searchers are specifically looking for your keywords.

Following are links for submission to some of the major search engines in no particular order. (Search engines are constantly changing. If these links don't work, go to the main site page and look for "submit" or "add a site.")

MSN Live Search
http://search.msn.com/docs/submit.aspx?FORM=WSDD2

Accoona
http://www.accoona.com/public/submit_website.jsp

AltaVista
http://addurl.altavista.com/addurl/default

Searchit
http://www.searchit.com/addurl.htm

DMOZ - Open Directory Project
http://www.dmoz.org/add.html

Google
http://www.google.com/addurl/?continue=/addurl

Lycos
http://sponsoredlistings.ask.com/lycos/

Yahoo
https://siteexplorer.search.yahoo.com/submit

AllTheWeb
http://www.alltheweb.com/help/webmaster/submit_site

Dogpile
http://www.enhance.com/dogpile.html

GigaBlast
http://www.gigablast.com/addurl

All the above are typical search engines except DMOZ which is also known as the Open Directory Project. The URLs that make it into this directory are manually inserted by human editors who review each page that webmasters submit. There's no computer robot involved here. The editors will recognize and delete deliberate spam submissions. They will usually use the title and keywords you submit. But they will delete repetitious phrases and misleading keywords. You'll find guidelines for submission at: http://www.dmoz.org/help/submit.html.

Open Directory ranks its sites by what is in the title, description, and category. Best of all, it powers directory listings for Netscape, Google, AltaVista, Lycos, AOL, and others. That means one submission to the ODP may get you into the search results for all these engines. One drawback - getting listed is notoriously slow since you have to wait for overworked human editors to cull through thousands of other submissions before yours, and this may take 6-8 weeks. Being in the Open Directory is somewhat like a "badge of honor" for your site that will bring positive benefits for many years.

Link Lists

The *Persian Kitty* site was mentioned in a previous chapter as an example of the link list. These are excellent sources of traffic - probably only second to search engines. You know the surfer is looking for porn or he wouldn't be at the link list site. The webmasters running the list are careful to screen out inferior sites so the quality of their offerings will attract more viewers. To refresh your memory, link lists contain links (URLs) that connect to complete websites along with a short text description next to each link. They link to small free sites consisting of a few pages with banner ads. Usually there is a warning page as the first page followed by the main page. The main page will contain 2-4 links to gallery pages.

I've had tremendous success with *Persian Kitty* (PK) over the years. Go to (http://www.persiankitty.com and let's use it as an example. At the top of the page beneath the logo is a warning in small font text. Interspersed throughout the page are several large banners advertising various pay sites. Some of these are about half the screen height in size (known as half-page banners). *Persian Kitty* gets paid the webmaster's commission if anyone clicks on these banners and joins the membership site. Further down is a box called the "Jumpstation" that contains text links to various other pages by category. These pages are also run by *Persian Kitty*. Skip down through a couple more banners and you'll find an alphabetical listing of sites. This is the heart of the link list. The newest submissions are listed at the top along with the submission date. Older submissions follow, and they may remain on the site for months depending upon how well PK likes the site. Another feature of this site is the automatic rotation of the site names by letters of the alphabet. Sites beginning with the letter "A" stay at the top about four days. Then they get bumped to the bottom of the list and the "B"s move to the top. This is more than fair as it insures that all webmasters get a shot at the top placement. I have found the number of hits received from PK varies greatly depending upon how high you are on the list. Even at the bottom, though, you'll still get a significant amount of traffic.

Now go back to the Jumpstation box and find the link marked "Submit/Update a link". This is where you will submit your site. Looking at the submission form will acquaint you with the rules for this site which are typical. (Rules vary slightly for each link list so always check before submitting.)

Note that you must have a "real email address" as PK calls it - not a free email account. I've explained that in a previous chapter. For a free site with pictures you need at least 30 free pics, movies, and/or stories. This requirement might be met by two galleries of sixteen photos each. Note that you must put a Persian Kitty banner or text link on your site in order to be accepted, and PK offers a number of free banners. There is usually a requirement that the link be on one of the first pages and fairly high on the page so it can be seen without scrolling down. It may seem strange to be asking for a link back to the same page that the surfer just came from, but this is a standard of the business. Click the Listing Requirements link for more rules. Note that sites on free hosts are not accepted. Nor are sites on overloaded servers that don't respond fast enough. Sites that in any way suggest child porn are taboo. PK specifically forbids words such as "lolita", "babies", "young", or "schoolgirls". (Teens, college girls, or coeds are acceptable, though, since they are standards in the adult business.) Another universal rule is no popup or exit consoles allowed. You've seen these plenty of times even on legitimate sites - windows that pop up over or under the main window with advertising for something. This sums up the most important rules. None of these will cramp your style, and strict adherence will earn you repeat acceptances of you sites and top notch traffic in return.

Thumbnail Gallery Post

The TGP has already been discussed in an earlier chapter. Here you submit a single gallery page to the TGP. It has about sixteen thumbnails linked to full-size images along with about two banners or text links promoting pay sites. Often, a single gallery promotes just one pay site with a banner at the top and complementary text links at the bottom. Like the link list, there is a requirement for a link back to the TGP site. This can be in the form of a small banner image provided by the TGP or a text link. For some reason never clear to me, it is common to require that the page have three reciprocal links to TGP sites. I've never figured out this rationale since they're actually requiring you to put up some links for their competitors. So it is common to find three thumbnail sized links at the bottom of the page. You would submit the same gallery to each of those TGP sites. Then you'd make another copy of the same gallery, paste on links for another three TGP sites and submit to them, too. So one gallery page might be copied into six files which will ultimately get submitted to eighteen different TGPs.

When your page first gets added to the TGP site, you'll get thousands of hits the first day - maybe even tens of thousands of hits. In subsequent days, your link will be rotated further down on the list, and the hits will decline. Your link will be deleted after a week or two. This is really a never ending process with TGP submissions. Some guys build one or more galleries per day and submit them to two dozen sites. You can even buy specialized software programs for gallery submissions.

I mentioned that search engines provide the best quality of traffic followed by link lists. "Quality" refers to the type of surfer who comes to your site, and his potential for becoming the member of a pay site. After all, you don't make a cent unless the surfer joins. The secret is to find guys who are looking for the quality of content that pay sites offer and also happen to have a credit card to be used to purchase a membership. This leaves out persons in many third-world countries and those who are under the legal age to have credit cards. You could market to thousands of high school boys and never get a sale. Think about that...they don't have credit cards. What you want is to market to twenty-somethings and up who have the money to spend and the desire to join.

The quality of hits from TGPs is generally considered to be much poorer. Most of the surfers using TGP sites are just looking for free porn. They go from site to site each day taking in all the offerings with never a thought of making a purchase. Therefore, you have to have a tremendous number of hits from TGPs to result in a single purchase. Keep this in mind as you schedule your efforts. Ten thousand hits from a TGP might produce a single buyer whereas only one thousand from a link list or one hundred from a search engine may give the same results. So always keep in mind the quality of your traffic.

Doorway Page

This is somewhat unique. It is a single advertising page that you submit to search engines. The page is a marketing tool to try to get the surfer to go to a single pay site. It may have a photo or two and some banners for the site or it may have a half-page ad provided by the sponsor. But mainly it's got text copy that convinces the surfer to click on the link to go to the pay site. In order to be successful the page needs to be optimized very well for search engines and that means a lot of appropriate text for the keywords involved. There are a lot of doorway pages on the net - not just for porn. Just think how many times you clicked on a URL that took you to a one page site that extolled the virtues of some product and then routed you to the product's main website. You can create numerous doorway pages that link to your affiliate sponsors and submit them to search engines. As you can see, your traffic really comes from search engines and your doorway serves as an intermediary stop where you can future promote the pay site.

Traffic Brokers

I have never personally used a traffic broker. Here you purchase a certain number of hits from the broker. For example, the broker agrees to route you 10,000 hits for an agreed price. Traffic brokers exist for both adult and non-adult websites. Where the traffic comes from is the problem. If traffic is coming from non-adult areas of the web, then probably those surfers are not going to be in the mood to buy porn. Adult brokers will generally route you traffic from other adult sites - particularly free sites and TGPs. These routing sites may have general links somewhere on their pages that say "Click here for more porn" or something link that. The problem is the poor quality of traffic which is probably a lot of guys looking for free porn. Another common complaint is that the broker did not supply the agreed number of hits. Guess who does the counting? The broker has a program that counts the links he is sending you. Unfortunately, the number of surfers that actually connect and view your site may not match the broker's count. This may be physical problems with the net or it may even be problems with your site. Fortunately, broker traffic contracts are almost always short term. You can try it once or twice and see what you think. Always bear in mind that the bottom dollar is how many memberships you are able to sell from this traffic.

Hardware and Software

This chapter will review how our workflow will proceed and the hardware and software needed. There is nothing complex about the requirements. There are many alternatives with regard to software - both purchased commercial products and downloadable freeware or shareware.

Workflow

1. Design a free site containing several galleries and multiple sponsors' banners.

2. Test the site on your own computer. There are a couple of ways to do this. Simple tests can be done by opening the Warning Page within your browser and clicking through each of the site links to test them. Click on the link for the Main Page, then each Gallery Page. A better way to test is to run program that creates your own local web server on your computer. The URL for this server is named "localhost" so typing just that word into your browser's URL entry line should bring up your site. (This assumes that you have the local server program running in the background.) There are a lot of these small server programs available on the web and many are free. The one I use is *Simple Server* - a free download from AnalogX:

Simple Server
http://www.analogx.com/contents/download/network/sswww.htm

As its name implies, this is very simple and easy to use. Download it and give it a try. Just set up a simple index.htm file that will be your homepage for testing. It can say something like "Hello World - Welcome to my website." Once the server is configured and running, type "localhost" into your browser and see your hello world message pop up. Here is the HTML code for a simple test page:

```
<HTML>
<BODY>
<CENTER><H1>Hello World<BR>Welcome to my website!</H1></CENTER>
</BODY>
```

3. With your site thoroughly tested on your local computer, use a file transfer (FTP) program to move the files to your hosted website. "FTP" stands for file transfer protocol, a method of moving files about the Internet. There are numerous FTP programs available and many are free or shareware. Shareware programs usually cost up to $50 but they often have "light" versions available for free. You don't need much more than the basic features in any of these FTP programs. We'll discuss WS-FTP below since it is one of the most popular.

4. Test the pages on your hosted website. Make sure all the links are working. Be sure to click the sponsors' banners to make sure that go to the intended pay sites. Now you're ready for business and need to attract surfers.

5. Submit your site to search engines and link lists. Follow the suggestions in the chapter on traffic.

6. Monitor your site on a regular basis. You may want to download a free counter program that keeps track of the number of visitors. Put the counter at the bottom of your warning page and follow the instructions for displaying your stats. (Your hosting company may also have free counters available.) You don't need a counter on every page - we're mainly interested only in the total number of visitors who hit the first page. Multiple-page counters can be helpful in some

instances. For example, suppose you get 1000 hits per day on your Warning Page, but only 300 on your Main Page. This might indicate that surfers are immediately going to your affiliate sponsors' pay sites. On the other hand, it might indicate that surfers are rejecting your site because the Warning Page doesn't entice them to go further. Or maybe your "Click here to enter" link is so hidden that surfers miss it completely.

7. Once you start getting hits on your site, go to each pay site's affiliate area and look up your statistics. Stats should show how many users have clicked through to the pay site and any sales.

Hardware

1. Your home or office computer with a fast Internet connection is sufficient for your adult website. It is assumed that you are running any recent version of Microsoft Windows. Don't try running an adult site with a telephone line and modem. With the large file sizes used, it's just too slow. A cable modem or DSL line will work sufficiently.

2. Your web server will be the second computer. We assume this as a virtual server account located at some web hosting company far away from your location. The only thing you need to know about your web server is how to transfer a file to it via FTP. Some web hosts offer a choice of Windows or Linux hosting. This simply means whether your virtual server's operating system is some version of Windows or Linux which is a pc-based version of the Unix operating system. Most adult sites use Linux systems because they are usually thought to have faster operating response times. Linux-based hosting is usually cheaper, too, so it's a no-brainer. Just go with Linux. The only thing you need to remember with Linux is that file names are case sensitive whereas with Windows they are not. So "index.htm" and "Index.Htm" are different files on a Linux system. This can lead to exasperating problems where everything works on your local Windows computer, but there are broken links after you transfer the files to the Linux unit. A simple rule is to always keep your file names in lower case. Avoid mixed case or upper case.

Software

1. There may be issues as to whether you want your family or co-workers to see the files for an adult site so you may need to take some measures to hide your work. There are actually password protected programs that can be used to hide whole directories of files. One of the most popular that I use regularly is *Magic Folders*, a shareware product, which can be downloaded here:

Magic Folders

http://www.pc-magic.com/

This software is well worth the small cost if you need to hide your work from prying eyes. (Don't buy the encrypted version. It is too slow and not necessary for your purposes.)

2. A text editor or HTML editor is needed to write your source code. Windows comes with the built-in Notepad editor. Just go to the Start Button in Windows, click Run, and enter "notepad" in the box. This editor can be perfectly adequate for beginning websites. There are many freeware editors that have more advanced features than Notepad. The one I use is *NoteTab Lite* which is available here:

NoteTab Lite

http://www.notetab.com/ntl.php

This is a good example of a shareware product that also offers an excellent light version as freeware.

If you're not familiar with HTML coding, by all means buy one of the many beginners books. If possible, peruse though numerous books in any large bookstore. Some of the books have an accompanying CD-ROM disk that contains freeware editors. For example, "Building a Web Site for Dummies" has a companion CD-ROM containing evaluation versions of useful tools, such as *Paint Shop Pro, HomeSite , Fireworks,* and *Dreamweaver.*

There are also many downloadable editors at *download.com*. Just type "HTML Editor" in their search box. On that site, each software item also shows the total number of downloads. Choose one that has a large number of downloads. Most of these products are shareware but many have free trial periods, and some are free.

CNET Download.Com

http://www.download.com

Many HTML editors use the WYSIWYG approach which means "what you see is what you get." As you build your page, the editor displays exactly what it will look like in a separate window so you can instantly review the results of each change.

The CoffeeCup Free HTML Editor is a good example of this WSSIWYG technique. It's a drag and drop HTML Editor with built-in FTP uploading. It has wizards for tables, frames, forms and fonts and comes with all HTML tags. The Free version also includes wizards for images, links and a Quickstart so you can create web pages fast. You can download it here:

CoffeeCup Free HTML Editor

http://www.coffeecup.com/free-editor/

3. A code checker has been mentioned previously. These programs will flag syntax errors in your HTML code. They are life savers when you get into pages that have hundreds of lines of complex code. The one that I use is the freeware *CSE HTML Validator Lite* found at the following URL:

CSE HTML Validator Lite

http://www.htmlvalidator.com/lite/

4. A file transfer program (FTP) is essential to get files from your computer to your host's server. There are a number of freeware programs available, but I prefer one of the most popular shareware

products: *WS-FTP Home* available from Ipswitch software. The free trial version is good for 30 days and costs $39.95 to purchase at this URL:

WS-FTP Home

http://www.ipswitch.com/purchase/products/ws_ftp_home.asp

Some of the screens are shown below to explain the FTP process. This assumes that your site is on a server named "server01" on a host named "myhost.com," and your account name is "johndoe." All this information will be provided in the instructions from your hosting company.

Using WS-FTP, we'll click the Quick Connect button to demonstrate:

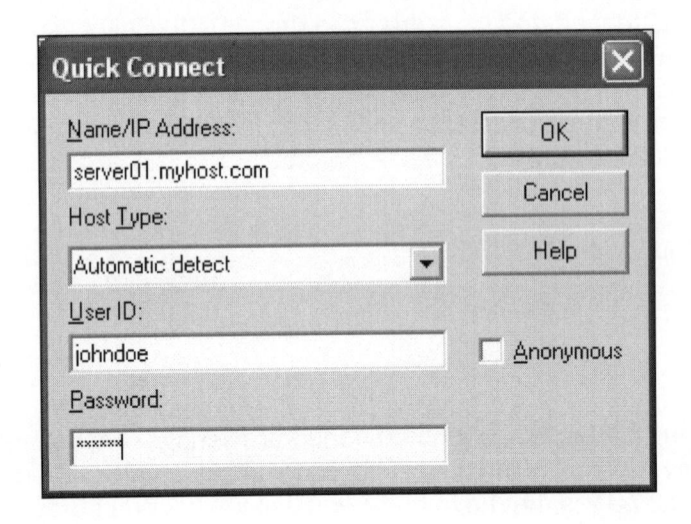

After logging in, you will see a screen with left and right panes as seen below. The left pane displays folders on your local computer. The right pane displays the folders on your webserver account. You will probably need to click through the folders in each pane until you find the hotsexygirls folder for each:

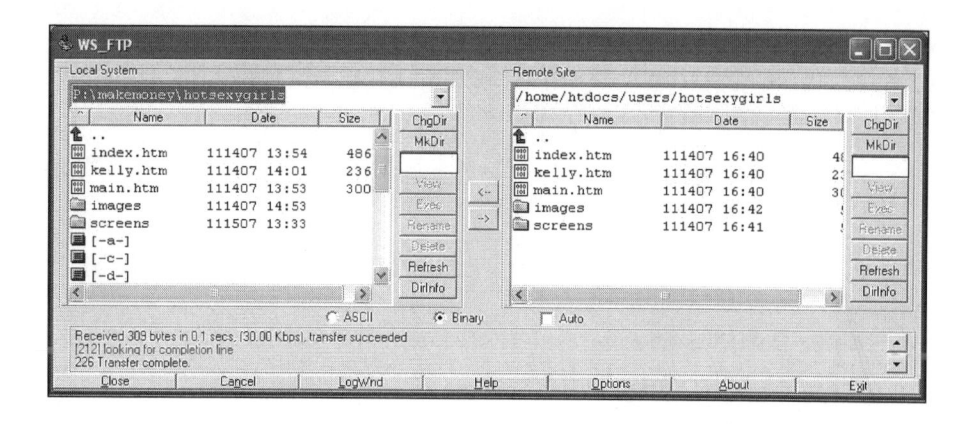

When you make your first file transfer, the remote site will have none of your files and you will need to create the directory to hold them. (Follow the instructions from your hosting company.) Use the MkDir button next to the right pane to create your directory. Then double-click on your new directory, and it should look something link the above screen but without the files. Now we need to transfer the files on the local computer (left pane) to the right. This can be done by double-clicking the left files or by highlighting them and clicking the right arrow button in the center of the screen. You'll see an informational message as the transfer occurs.

That completes the basic FTP process. Finally, use your browser to go to your site on the Internet and check your files. Look, especially, for any broken links or missing images. Remember that filenames in the right pane are generally case-sensitive so slight differences in capitalization of their names will result in broken links.

Other FTP programs work in a similar manner. You need to have your hosting account set up before trying FTP. Then you can download and try a couple of programs. Your web host may also have some suggestions for file transfer. You don't need a fancy piece of software for your FTP needs so don't spend a lot of money on versions with lots of extra features.

5. An image editor is essential, and there are so many available that we won't go into detail about any specific product. There are only a few features that you absolutely need. Many editors come bloated

with so many "professional" features that you would need a year just to learn how to use them. Keep it simple is the rule to follow. Here are the features you will need regularly:

(1) Resize images
(2) Crop images
(3) Create text for logos and custom banners
(4) Sharpen images
(5) Compress file size of images

The editor that most professional photographers and graphics artists use is *Adobe Photoshop* which costs over $600. There is absolutely no reason to spend money on a product like this. Adobe has a cheaper editor that I like, *Photoshop Elements*, which retails for around $100. *Paint Shop Pro* from Corel costs under $100 and is sometimes referred to as the "poor man's Photoshop" because it gives Adobe's premier product a good run for the money. If you have Microsoft Office, it comes with *Microsoft Photo Editor* that will be installed under Office Tools. If you go to any big retail store that sells software, you'll find at least half a dozen software titles under the general category of photo and imaging software. Competition is keen in this area because of the popularity of digital cameras so don't spend a fortune. Google even offers a free photo editor named *Picasa*.

Google Picasa
(http://picasa.google.com/).

A good source of image editors is the CNET site: http://www.download.com/. Type in "image editor" or "photo editor" in the search box at the top. You'll find hundreds of editors including some free ones. As you're just getting started in webmastering, take a day to search for an editor you'll be comfortable with. Look for one that's simple in design and easy to use. Try editing some photos of your own (most also come with sample images) and do each of the five actions listed above.

6. While not an image editor, *IrfanView* is a free graphic viewing product that is extremely popular. I use it the time to quickly browse through directories of images on my computer. It's much faster than opening a larger image editing program if you just want to view the images.

IrfanView

http://www.irfanview.net/.

7. File compression and decompression programs are a must but for the most part you won't need to spend any money as long as you have a recent copy of Windows. *PKZip* and *WinZip* are some of the standards of the industry. These use to have to be purchased separately but Windows now includes the *PKZip* software in its standard features. You won't really need to compress files unless you just want to cut down on the amount of space they take on your computer. However, many of the files that you download (software and image content) come as ZIP files that need to be uncompressed. (These are called "ZIP" files because they have the file extension ".zip" which is an industry standard.) Any modern version of Windows should take care of decompression automatically. Just right-click on the ZIP file and select the option to uncompress.

PKZip

(included in Windows)

WinZip

http://www.winzip.com/

8. As a beginner you probably won't need to do an image mapping. This involves creating clickable areas on a large image. You may often see this on commercial websites. Instead of clicking a real link or button, you click on a portion of the image to go to another page. This uses a HTML technique where the source code for the page contains certain mapped coordinates that will perform an action if the mouse is clicked in that area. Creating these maps requires some type of mapping software. You highlight or mark a portion of the image, and the software creates the necessary HTML code. Then you add this code to the appropriate web page. Your image editor may

contain this feature so check there first. Otherwise, there are a couple of inexpensive products to do the job.

MapEdit

http://boutel.com/mapedit/

CofeeCup Image Mapper

http://www.coffeecup.com/image-mapper/

Backing Up Your Site

If you hang out on the adult forums, you'll often hear tales of woe from guys who lost their website for some reason and have no backup. This happens so often that one wonders "how could they be so stupid?" There are several reasons you might lose your data:

1. Your hard drive fails or files become corrupted.
2. Your host's server hard drive fails or is otherwise corrupted.
3. You accidentally erase your files on your local or remote computer.
4. Your host cancels your account for some reason.

To prevent catastrophic loss you need to develop a philosophy about backing up date as well as a method. The live version of your site will exist on the server run by your hosting company. There should always be an exact copy on your computer located at your home or office. This would be the computer that your normally use to develop your site - the one from which you FTP your files back and forth to the server. It is truly amazing how many times guys who suffered huge loses will say they didn't have a local copy of their website. Your philosophy needs to be thus:

There will always be an up-to-date and complete copy of my website on my PC.

Many hosting companies offer tape backup services. There is often an additional monthly charge for these backups. Personally, I don't use them since my backup copy is always on my local computer. Hard drive space is so inexpensive nowadays that you can even use a separate external drive for backups.

With the amount of data that can be written to compact disks, small sites can be copied completely to a single disk. This has the advantage of being able to store different versions of your sites as they appeared on certain dates. Almost all modern PC computers have a read-write CD drive, and the cost of disks purchased in 50 or 100 packs is less that a quarter each. Don't use the CD read-write disks (CD-RW). They are less reliable and cost more. Read-only disks (CD-R) are fine and cost so little that they can be considered as throwaways when not needed.

Here is my recommended backup procedure:

1. Original site is on hosted web server.
2. Exact copy is on home or office PC.
3. CD copies of the sites on the PC will be made on a regular basis.
4. For a large number of sites, backup the files to an external hard drive.

Compact disk copies can be stored in a safe place away from your PC. Ideally, they might go in a fireproof safe or to an offsite location. Likewise, the external hard drive might be stored in a safe location away from your PC. Let's consider what will happen in an emergency:

Recently, one of my hosting companies sent an email to all the webmasters using a particular web server: "The hard drive on this server has failed. We will restore sites for those users having paid for tape backups. Other users will need to restore their own files." Their server was down for over a day. When it came back up, there was nothing but empty space in my account area. This would have been a disaster for many webmasters who don't follow a backup procedure. In my case I knew all the files would exist in the exact copy on my PC. Therefore, I used FTP transfer to copy all the files back to the new hard drive on the server. This wasn't too bad since I was able to copy an entire site at a time by simply setting the FTP program to copy the starting directory and all subdirectories.

A second hypothetical emergency might occur if the hard drive on your computer fails. Your website will continue to operate because it's on the remote server. You biggest problem will be getting your PC fixed or to purchase a new computer and get it configured with software. Hopefully, you will have the original install CDs for major software products. (For software you have downloaded, it's a good idea to keep copies of the original downloads stored way on CDs also.) Once your computer is restored, just log into your server account and use FTP to transfer all the files from your web server back to your PC. Now you've got the exact copy again. If this fails, you can restore your most recently backed-up version from a compact disk.

Having CD backups available is important for another reason. They give you a historical version of your site for legal purposes. Suppose you become involved in a legal dispute over some trademark or copyright issue. Your historical backups may show when you first starting using the material that is the subject of the legal dispute.

Taxes and Other Business Matters

Here's something most "how to get rich" books won't tell you: You have to pay income taxes on your profits. Assuming you are in the United States or most other civilized jurisdictions that collect taxes upon income, you will need to reveal your income and expenses at tax time. Income minus expenses = profit. You pay taxes on the profit. The form you'll need for this is one of the versions of Schedule C shown below. There are just a couple of points to consider:

The form asks for your "Principal business or profession." This refers only to the business you are operating to produce income reported on this form. You don't need to reveal that you are an adult webmaster. Here we need to consider what it is that you're really doing, and this will surprise you -- you're running an advertising service using the Internet. The whole purpose of your porn sites is not to amuse guys by getting them off. The real purpose is to serve as an advertising agent for your sponsors. You have contracts with those sponsors by virtue of your signup agreements. You're a businessman performing on those contracts by seeking out memberships for the sponsors' websites. I always answer this question by stating that my business is "Internet Advertising."

The form also asks you to enter a code taken from a listing of hundreds of codes in the instructions. This throws most guys because the codes don't include webmastering or porn. Look under the category "Other Professional, Scientific, & Technical Services" on the list, and you'll find "541800 - Advertising & related services." There you go. Use "541800" for the business code. See, you never had to reveal what you really do, and you're honestly answering the questions.

In the expense columns on the form, most of your expenses will fall in a readily identifiable category. The one exception is hosting expenses. Assuming you are using an external hosting company as I have recommended, what you're really doing is renting server space. These expenses can go in the column for "Rent or lease...Other business property." I have also listed hosting expenses under the last column titled "Other expenses." You probably don't want to list travel, meals, or car expenses unless you really have those, and they are directly related to this business. Let's not put up any red flags in the first year's taxes. However, if you attended an adult webmasters conference such as the annual InterNext-Expo in Las Vegas, those expenses might well be deductible. Check this link for more info:

Internext-Expo

http://www.internext-expo.com/

The full Schedule C forms are available from the IRS web site all year long. You can view or print them in PDF format.

Internal Revenue Service Forms

http://www.irs.ustreas.gov/

Form 1040 Schedule C - Profit or Loss from Business

This is the form used by most businesses that are owned by an individual who is considered to be a sole proprietor. My grandfather ran a hardware store. Since he owned the business outright, he was a sole proprietor. Unless you have incorporated your web business, formed a limited liability company, or formed a partnership, you will be considered a sole proprietor. Here you declare your gross income and expenses. This form is file as one page with the rest of your 1040 income tax form. (You may qualify for the simpler Schedule C-EZ shown later.)

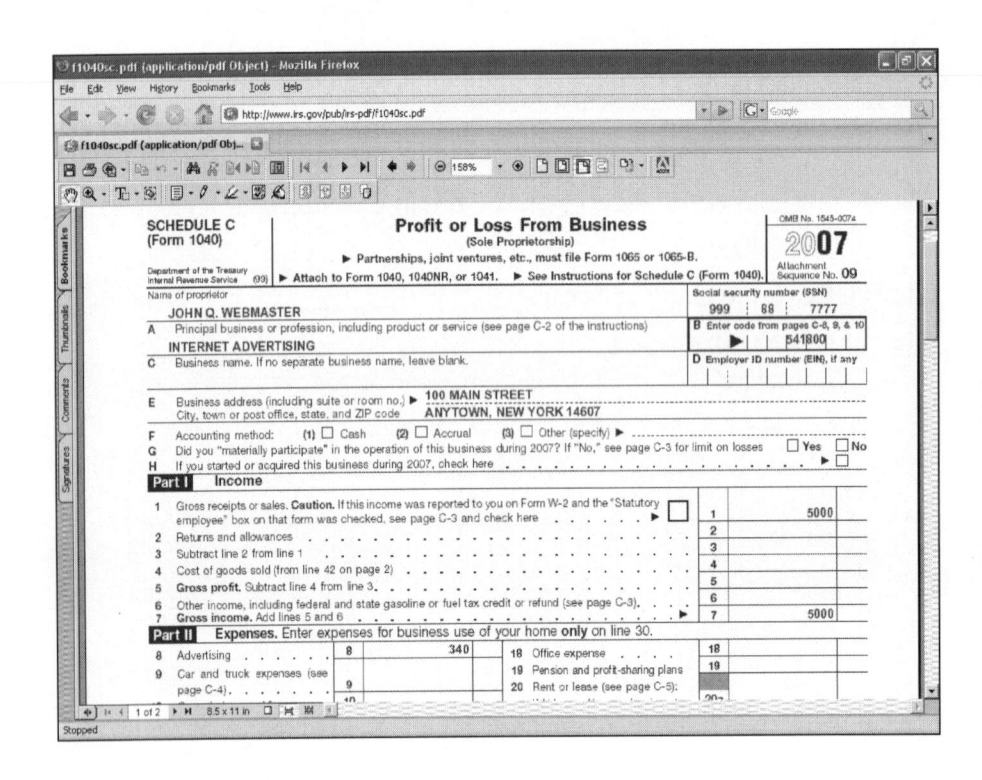

Form 1040 Schedule C-EZ

    You can use this simplified form if your business expenses were $5000 or less, did not have a net loss for the year, and had only one business as a sole proprietor. There are some other requirements to meet. If you qualify, this is the form to use.

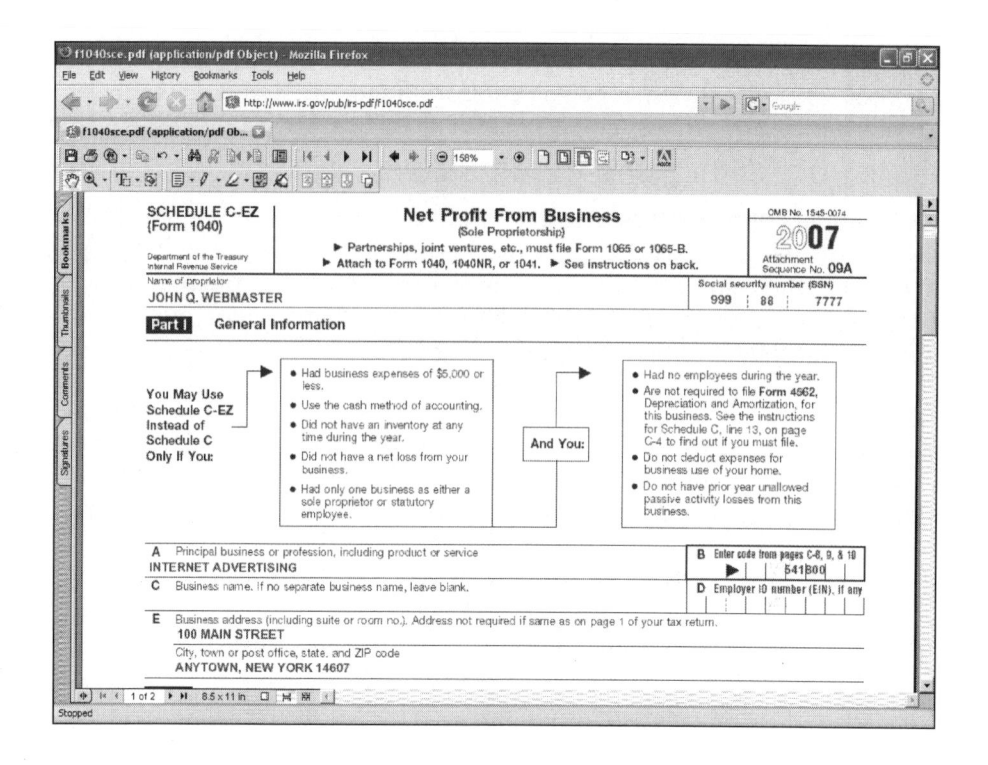

    Should you cheat on all of this and just not report to the tax man? If you're really not making much money, the government will probably never find out. On the other hand, keep in mind the for U.S. citizens, your sponsors are required to report your income to the IRS on Form 1099 if you were paid more than $600 in a year. Your sponsors will send you a copy of these forms if they have reported your income. If you get a 1099 form, you definitely have to report the income, or you'll be learning all about tax audits the hard way.

Glossary of Adult Terms

Affiliate - A person who enters into a contractual relationship with a sponsor whereby the affiliate will send traffic to the sponsor's websites in return for a commission on any sales generated.

AVS (Adult Verification System) - A method for verifying the age of surfers by using the AVS company as a middleman between the surfer and the adult web pages. This is connected to a payment scheme for the adult webmaster who makes a commission each time a surfer purchases entry to a site via the AVS.

Bandwidth - In web hosting, this is the amount of computer bytes used to transfer a page or image. For example, if a photo is 40,000 bytes in size, then the amount of bandwidth used to transfer the photo across the web to the surfer is 40,000 (40kb).

Banner Farm - A page or site that consists mostly of advertising banners with little real content.

Chargeback - This occurs where a credit card user has made a valid charge and later asks the credit card company to reverse the charge. This results in a credit to the card user and a debit (i.e. chargeback) to the merchant.

Dedicated Hosting - A hosting arrangement where the hosting company provides a separate server for the exclusive use of the webmaster who may pay a setup fee plus a monthly fee.

DMOZ - The URL of the Open Directory Project (dmoz.org)

Fake TGP - A site that appears to be a Thumbnail Gallery Post but doesn't really accept submissions from other webmasters. All the galleries featured in the links are actually posted by the operator of the fake site to generate profits from signups.

FPA - A full page ad that takes up the entire screen. This may be a very large banner or a combination of text and images or banners.

FTP (File Transfer Protocol) - A common method for transferring computer files about the Internet.

Geo-targeted Ad - This is an advertising method in which the approximate physical location is determined to reading the surfer's IP address and comparing that to a database of IP address locations. The specific ad will then be delivered customized for the geographical location. For example: a dating site might deliver ads to New Yorkers with text saying "Meet available girls in New York."

Gigabyte - One million bytes of transfer across the Internet. Also see Bandwidth.

HTML (Hypertext Markup Language) - The computer programming language commonly used to code web pages for the Internet.

Hotlinking - This occurs when a webmaster cheats by linking his site to content (especially photos) that are on another webmaster's site without permission.

ICANN (Internet Corporation for Assigned Names and Numbers) - The organization responsible for the global coordination of the Internet's system of unique identifiers including domain names (like .org, .museum and country codes like .UK) as well as the addresses used in a variety of Internet protocols.

InterNIC - Provides public information regarding domain registration and services. The InterNIC website is operated by ICANN.

Javascript - A computer programming language often used on web pages. This is usually inserted into the page's header and is not seen by the viewer. It enables various activities that would not be possible with ordinary HTML coding.

Keyword - In search engine terminology, these are important words found on a web page that describe the content of the page. Keywords are combined into key phrases. When a surfer types words into the search box on a search engine, the desired words are used to lookup similar phrases in the search engines database.

Link List - A type of adult site that features categorized links to many different porn sites but does not actually display images from the linked sites. The linked sites are usually free sites.

Merchant Account - A contractual arrangement for the use of its credit card charging system between a bank and a merchant. For example: a large pay site might have a merchant account with a bank so as to accept its Visa credit cards.

Niche - A type of adult site content that does not fall into the more general categories (hardcore, softcore, teens, amateurs.) For example: big boobs, mature, asses.

Open Directory Project (ODP) - A very large and comprehensive human-edited directory of the Web. It is constructed and maintained by a vast, global community of volunteer editors. The URL of its search website is *dmoz.org*.

PageRank - Google's term for a method of ranking the quality of pages in its database according to content and link popularity.

Pay Per Click (PPC) - A payment arrangement in which the affiliate webmaster is paid a small amount each time a surfer clicks through to a sponsor's pay site.

Pay Per Signup - A payment method in which the affiliate webmaster is paid a set fee each time a surfer clicks through to a sponsor's pay site and purchases a membership.

Pay Site - An adult site that charges surfers for the right to view its content. Charges are usually based on a monthly membership fee.

Ratio - A method of describing the number of clicks by surfers that is required to produce a sale of the product. For example: a ratio of 50/10000 would mean that there are 50 sales for every 10,000 clicks.

Rebill - A common billing arrangement where the surfer purchases a monthly membership that will be automatically billed again each month until such time as the purchaser chooses to cancel.

Recurring Membership - See Rebill.

Registrar - An organization (usually for-profit) that handles registration of domain names. Registrars are accredited and regulated by ICANN.

Robot - A computer program used by search engines to traverse the World Wide Web reading web pages for various sites and categorizing them into a database. The robot (or spider) follows each link on the web page to find more pages deeper in the site or on other external sites.

SERP (Search Engine Results Page) - This is the page that a search engine delivers back to the surfer who has submitted a search request. It will consist of a listing of site URLs that match the keywords the surfer has submitted.

Shaving - An undesirable practice by some sponsor programs that undercount the number of clicks or sales that are attributable to a specific affiliate webmaster. This is considered to be cheating.

Spider - See Robot.

Sponsor - A company offering affiliate programs for its pay sites. The sponsor contracts with outside independent webmasters who become "affiliates." Each affiliate sends traffic to the sponsor's sites in return for a commission. Many sponsors nowadays have a dozen or more sites to promote.

Subdomain - A method for splitting up a single domain into multiple areas that appear as separate sites. For example: a main URL named "hotsexygirls.com" might have subdomains named "lesbians.hotsexygirls.com" and "coeds.hotsexygirls.com." Each subdomain can be addressed separately by its URL.

Third-Party Processor - A company that handles credit card processing under contract with a sponsor. It receives membership payments and maintains a Merchant Account with a credit card issuing bank. Payments are split between the sponsor and its affiliate webmaster according to the agreed terms.

Thumbnail Gallery Post (TGP) - A website featuring links to galleries that consist of thumbnail images. Clicking on the individual thumbs will lead to full-sized photos of the same subject. These are usually large sites with hundreds of links changed daily.

Turnkey Site - A web site that is sold as a complete and functional, operating site usually including hosting. It usually includes interactive scripts for forms, shopping carts, affiliate programs, etc. The buyer just "turns the key" so to speak in order to get started.

Virtual Hosting - A hosting plan that puts multiple web sites onto a shared single server. Each site appears by itself when its URL is typed into a browser. This is a generally inexpensive method of hosting for small sites.

Whois - An Internet program that displays information about a URL registration from the InterNIC database.

WYSIWYG (What you see is what you get) - A type of HTML editing program that displays web pages as they will look rather than in computer scripted code. During editing, the content appears to look very similar to the final product.

2257 - Refers to section 2257 of the United States Code which deals with child pornography. It places certain requirements on producers of adult materials to insure that all models are over eighteen years of age.

Getting Help

The adult webmaster community has been very easy going about giving free advice to new webmasters. There seems to always have been a feeling that the marketplace is big enough for all of us. In addition, there are many general purpose sites that deal with various facets of the Internet. Rather than a detailed discussion of these sources of help, I'll just list some of the best sites that I personally use categorized by the type of information provided. There is one caveat - I suggest that you do not spend a lot of time in adult discussion groups as I've found that, while entertaining, this is generally a waste of time. It is much better to peruse the sites listed below that can help you achieve concrete results with a minimum of chat.

Due to the ever changing nature of the Internet, some of the URLs below may cease to work as sites come and go, but they are accurate as of this writing in fall of 2007. You can also use a search engine to do further research on any number of topics - for example: "adult web hosting." There are so many sites available that I will try to only loosely categorize them and leave it to you to search out each site.

WhoIs Sites

Lookup the site registration and ownership information

Network Solutions Whois
http://www.networksolutions.com/whois/
Psychic Whois

http://www.psychicwhois.com/

Domain Tools
> http://www.domaintools.com/

Who.Is
> http://www.whois.ws/

Access Whois
> http://www.accesswhois.com/search/

Better-Whois
> http://www.betterwhois.com/

Search Engine Sites

Optimization and submission advice

WebProWorld Search Engine Forums
> http://www.webproworld.com/index.php

WebSiteOptimization.Com
> http://www.websiteoptimization.com/

WebWorkshop
> http://www.webworkshop.net/

SearchEngineWatch
> http://searchenginewatch.com/

SearchEngineWatch Forums
> http://forums.searchenginewatch.com/index.php

High Rankings Forums
> http://www.highrankings.com/forum/

Domain Registration

Register your domain with one of these companies.

DirectNic
> http://www.directnic.com/

Register.com
> http://www.register.com/

GoDaddy.com
> http://www.godaddy.com/

Web Hosting

Hosting companies and directories of hosts. Be sure the host accepts adult sites.

TopHosts
> http://www.tophosts.com/

HostIndex
> http://www.hostindex.com/

HostSearch
> http://hostsearch.com/

Blue Gravity
> http://www.bluegravity.com

WebAir
> http://www.webair.com

Adult TopHosts
> http://adult.tophosts.com/

Hosts4Porn
> http://www.hosts4porn.com/

Programming Tools

All kinds of tools and utilities to make your life easier

W3C Link Checker
  http://validator.w3.org/checklink
Keyword Extractor
  http://www.analogx.com/contents/download/network/keyex.htm

Whois Ultra
  http://www.analogx.com/contents/download/network/whois.htm
HyperTrace
  http://www.analogx.com/contents/download/network/htrace.htm

Freeware and Shareware Programs

Find all kinds of cheap or free software at these sites.

Freeware-Guide
  http://www.freeware-guide.com/
Freeware Home
  http://www.freewarehome.com/
CNET Download.com
  http://www.download.com/

Adult Webmaster Sites

All kinds of information and forums for adult webmasters.

Porn Resource

http://www.pornresource.com/

YNOT
http://www.ynot.com/

Adult Video News (AVN)
http://www.avn.com/

XBIZ
http://www.xbiz.com/

Cozy Frog
http://www.cozyfrog.com/

Web Overdrive
http://www.weboverdrive.com/

The Link Machine
http://www.thelinksmachine.com/

GreenGuy and Jim
http://www.greenguyandjim.com/

Newbie Webmasters
http://www.newbiewebmasters.com/

Netpond
http://www.netpond.com/

Adult Paysite Reviews

Use these sites to evaluate potential pay site sponsor programs.

Adult Reviews
http://adultreviews.net/

Sir Rodney's Porn Reviews
http://www.sirrodney.com/

Rabbit's Reviews
http://www.rabbitsreviews.com/

Adult Site Surfer
> http://adultsitesurfer.com/

The Best Porn
> http://www.thebestporn.com/home.html

Website Design

All kinds of topics to help you with designing your site.

The Site Wizard
> http://www.thesitewizard.com/

Adult Discussion Forums

Good advice (sometimes) and lots of opinions.

Adult Net Surprise
> http://www.adultnetsurprise.com/

PornCity Messageboard
> http://bbs.porncity.net/

Go Fuck Yourself
> http://www.gofuckyourself.com/

Another Adult Board
> http://www.anotheradultboard.com/board/

Cozy Campus Forums
> http://www.cozycampus.com/theforum/

Adult Content

Buy photos and video for your website content.

Paul Markham Content
> http://www.paulmarkham.com/

Bargain Basement Content
> http://www.bargainbasementcontent.com/

Amateur Cutie Content
> http://www.amateur-cutie-content.com/

Web-Legal Content
> http://www.web-legal.com/

FalconFoto
> http://www.falconfoto.com/

AdultContent.ca
> http://www.adultcontent.ca/

AdultContent.co.uk
> http://www.adultcontent.co.uk/

Adult Czech Content
> http://www.adultczechcontent.com/

Adult Industry Law

Legal resource sites specializing in adult industry law. Each is run by a prominent adult lawyer listed in parenthesis.

Adult Site Law (Anthony Compretto)
> http://www.adultsitelaw.com

Free Speech Law (Lawrence G. Walters)
> http://www.freespeechlaw.com

XXXLaw.Net (J.D. Obenberger)
> http://xxxlaw.net

Adult Industry Organizations

ASACP (Adult Sites Against Child Pornography)
> http://www.asacp.org

The Free Speech Coalition
> http://www.freespeechcoalition.com

Journals, Magazines, and Periodicals

There is one excellent monthly adult trade industry publication. *XBiz World* s the industry's first large-format trade publication, with a focus on business news, market trends, growth sectors, and international news in the online, offline, mobile and more. It is available on a free subscription basis if you can get signed up. That means the journal is free and mailed to you each month with the cost paid for by the advertisers. The only problem is that in order to sign up for a free subscription, you have to be an adult webmaster and list your URL in the application. Still, it's worth a try. If you can't get signed up, read the latest issue online and the following URL:

XBiz World Subscription
> http://www.xbizworld.com/

XBiz World Digital Edition
> http://xbiz.com/digital/

Printed in Great Britain
by Amazon